POVERTY AND ECONOMIC INEQUALITY

By Meghan Sharif

Portions of this book originally appeared in *Poverty* by Tina Kafka.

LUCENT
P R E S S

Published in 2019 by
Lucent Press, an Imprint of Greenhaven Publishing, LLC
353 3rd Avenue
Suite 255
New York, NY 10010

Designer: Andrea Davison-Bartolotta
Editor: Jennifer Lombardo

Library of Congress Cataloging-in-Publication Data

Names: Sharif, Meghan, author.
Title: Poverty and economic inequality / Meghan Sharif.
Description: New York : Lucent Press, [2019] | Series: Hot topics | Includes
  bibliographical references and index.
Identifiers: LCCN 2017058899| ISBN 9781534563537 (library bound book) | ISBN
  9781534563551 (pbk. book) | ISBN 9781534563544 (ebook)
Subjects: LCSH: Poverty–Juvenile literature. | Income distribution–Juvenile
  literature.
Classification: LCC HC79.P6 S535 2019 | DDC 339.4/6–dc23
LC record available at https://lccn.loc.gov/2017058899

Printed in the United States of America

CPSIA compliance information: Batch #BS18KL: For further information contact Greenhaven Publishing LLC, New York, New York at 1-844-317-7404.

Please visit our website, www.greenhavenpublishing.com. For a free color catalog of all our high-quality books, call toll free 1-844-317-7404 or fax 1-844-317-7405.

CONTENTS

Adolescence is a time when many people begin to take notice of the world around them. News channels, blogs, and talk radio shows are constantly promoting one view or another; very few are unbiased. Young people also hear conflicting information from parents, friends, teachers, and acquaintances. Often, they will hear only one side of an issue or be given flawed information. People who are trying to support a particular viewpoint may cite inaccurate facts and statistics on their blogs, and news programs present many conflicting views of important issues in our society. In a world where it seems everyone has a platform to share their thoughts, it can be difficult to find unbiased, accurate information about important issues.

It is not only facts that are important. In blog posts, in comments on online videos, and on talk shows, people will share opinions that are not necessarily true or false, but can still have a strong impact. For example, many young people struggle with their body image. Seeing or hearing negative comments about particular body types online can have a huge effect on the way someone views himself or herself and may lead to depression and anxiety. Although it is important not to keep information hidden from young people under the guise of protecting them, it is equally important to offer encouragement on issues that affect their mental health.

The titles in the Hot Topics series provide readers with different viewpoints on important issues in today's society. Many of these issues, such as teen pregnancy and Internet safety, are of immediate concern to young people. This series aims to give readers factual context on these crucial topics in a way that lets them form their own opinions. The facts presented throughout also serve to empower readers to help themselves or support people they know who are struggling with many of the challenges adolescents face today. Although negative viewpoints are not ignored or downplayed, this series allows young people to see that the challenges they face are not insurmountable. Eating disorders can be overcome, the Internet can be navigated safely, and pregnant teens do not have to feel hopeless.

Quotes encompassing all viewpoints are presented and cited so readers can trace them back to their original source, verifying for themselves whether the information comes from a reputable place. Additional books and websites are listed, giving readers a starting point from which to continue their own research. Chapter questions encourage discussion, allowing young people to hear and understand their classmates' points of view as they further solidify their own. Full-color photographs and enlightening charts provide a deeper understanding of the topics at hand. All of these features augment the informative text, helping young people understand the world they live in and formulate their own opinions concerning the best way they can improve it.

What Is Poverty?

When people hear the word "poverty," they may picture commercials they have seen on television, asking for donations for starving children who live far away. They may think of a neighborhood in their hometown full of broken-down or abandoned houses. They may think about not having enough to eat, not having a place to live, or a life without electricity or running water. All of these things are part of what poverty means, but the definition is complex. If someone does not have enough money to buy a new video game they really want, is that poverty? What if they have enough money to buy some food, but not healthy food they enjoy? The line that defines poverty is a matter of debate, and it differs from place to place.

While finding the exact definition of poverty may be difficult, everyone agrees that poverty is a serious global problem. Where poverty exists, people suffer. If people do not have enough money or resources to take care of their basic needs, they may go hungry, get sick and be unable to afford medicine, or not have a safe place to live. The more people living in poverty in an area, the more likely it is that contagious diseases will spread. Although it is difficult to see other people suffer in poverty, it is a problem that does not have an easy or quick solution.

Poverty creates a cycle, which means poverty leads to more poverty. If people are sick because they do not have access to food or medicine, it is hard for them to be able to work to earn money for the food and medicine they need. If people lose their homes, the lack of safe shelter leads to even more problems. If children grow up in families where they do not have enough to eat or a safe place to live, they are less likely to be able to stay in school; they may fail their classes because instead of studying and paying attention in class, they are worried about where their next meal is coming from. If these children do not get an education, it becomes even harder for them to grow up and make more money than their parents, and they can become trapped in this cycle of poverty.

Although it is a difficult problem to tackle, that has not stopped many organizations around the world from trying to fight and eliminate poverty. The United Nations (UN) and the World Bank, along with many nonprofit agencies, work in some of the most impoverished countries to try to lift people out of the cycle of poverty so they can lead healthier and more successful lives. With the technological advances of the 21st century, people are more aware of what goes on in places near and far. Some of this new technology has helped a great deal in the war against poverty, but there is still much work to be done.

Furthermore, there is a great deal of disagreement about what causes poverty and what the most effective solution will be. No one has yet found a perfect solution to help people, communities, or countries escape from the clutches of poverty, but there are some strategies that have been found to help. The more societies understand about the cycle of poverty, the more likely they are to be able to overcome the worst of its ill effects and the more likely it is that the world will become a more economically equal place.

CHAPTER 1

Determining Poverty

In order to fight poverty, one has to define it. While this sounds easy enough, it is actually very difficult—the definition of what counts as poverty and what does not is different from place to place. If someone has $1,000, are they poor or rich? It is hard to say because it depends on where the person lives, how much basic necessities cost there, and how much money the other people in their community have. In order to decide what counts as poverty and what does not, experts have come up with the poverty line.

The poverty line, or poverty threshold, is generally defined as the minimum level of income necessary to maintain a decent standard of living, either within one country or region or worldwide. Poverty lines are adjusted periodically to account for changes in the cost of living. For example, until 2008, the World Bank, an institution that provides financial assistance to the poorest countries, set the poverty line at $1 a day for people living in the poorest countries. In effect, people who lived on $1 or less were considered to be living in extreme poverty. That figure, however, was based on prices for goods and services in 1993. In 2004, using that measure, 985 million people worldwide lived below the poverty line. In 2008, the World Bank raised the international poverty line to $1.25. The change reflected updated costs of living. As surprising as it may seem, that small increase meant that 430 million more people were below the new poverty line. In 2015, the figure was raised again to its current $1.90 per day to recognize the growing costs of basic necessities.

There are different ways to determine poverty lines. This is important because the way poverty is measured changes the way

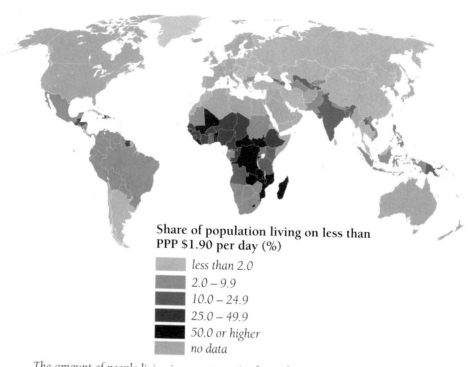

Share of population living on less than PPP $1.90 per day (%)

- less than 2.0
- 2.0 – 9.9
- 10.0 – 24.9
- 25.0 – 49.9
- 50.0 or higher
- no data

The amount of people living in poverty varies from place to place, as this World Bank information from 2013 shows. Purchasing power parity (PPP) defines the amount of goods and services that can be bought in each country with the equivalent of $1.90. The actual amount varies; for instance, something that costs $1.90 in England may cost $4 in the United States.

governments and organizations handle their anti-poverty programs. Douglas Besharov, formerly of the American Enterprise Institute for Public Policy Research, explained in a 2001 interview how changing the poverty line affects poverty programs in the United States. After the United States Census 2000, experts disagreed about whether to raise the poverty line to reflect changing incomes and prices. According to Besharov, "There is a political battle, a minor skirmish, going on here … with a number of people favoring the new measure because it would raise the count of poor and thus the need for more programs and more spending."[1] In the United States, being able to collect benefits such as food stamps, welfare, and government-funded health care depends on which side of the poverty line people fall.

The organization that oversees the global battle on poverty is the UN. The UN was founded after World War II to provide security to the nations of the world and to keep world peace. It has 193 member countries as of 2018. It functions as command central to coordinate many organizations that promote peace, safeguard the environment, and provide disaster relief and economic assistance to those in need.

The World Bank is one of the organizations that operates under the umbrella of the UN. The World Bank is not a bank in the traditional sense—it is an international institution that provides financial and technical assistance to developing countries. Most of its financial assistance takes the form of low-interest loans. The World Bank consists of 189 member countries. They work together to promote health care, education, agriculture, building of infrastructure, and sound financial management for countries that need support.

The World Bank carries out thousands of projects in every poverty-plagued region of the globe. In fiscal year 2017 (from July 1, 2016, to June 30, 2017), the World Bank loaned around $59 billion to fight poverty. Between 1947 and 2017, it has been involved in more than 13,087 projects in 173 different countries. The World Bank does not operate alone. Donor countries, which are member countries that have the resources to loan money, provide funds at low interest rates, and the bank partners with governments, communities, and private businesses on projects to help the poor.

Absolute Poverty

Poverty is generally discussed in terms of absolute poverty and relative poverty. Absolute measures of poverty determine a poverty line or threshold and then count the number of people who fall below that line. Measures of absolute poverty consider basic products and services people need to live. These include food, shelter, clean water, sanitation, and access to basic health care and education. The assumption behind measures of absolute poverty is that regardless of where people live, their basic needs are essentially the same.

No matter where someone lives, not having enough food to eat is a measure of poverty.

How many Americans live on $2 per day?
average number of households with children living on $2 per person per day, 1996-2011

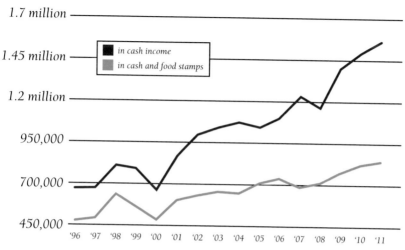

This information from the National Poverty Center shows the number of Americans living near the poverty line. Food stamps—money the government gives impoverished people to help them buy food—are included in this calculation.

There are benefits to measuring poverty in this way. Absolute poverty measures apply the same standards across cultures, geographic locations, and time periods. Therefore, absolute measures help experts compare standards of living around the world and over time. However, absolute measures do not account for the reality that resources, needs, and costs are not the same everywhere. For example, people who live in cold climates require a source of heat during the winter, whereas people on tropical islands do not. Heat requires energy, and that costs money that people in warm climates do not need to spend. This is why people who live in different areas cannot always be judged by the same standards.

To try to address these issues, David Gordon, a professor of social justice and director of the Townsend Centre for International Poverty Research at the University of Bristol in England, prepared a report for the United Nations in 2005 to help clarify absolute poverty. Gordon elaborated on the UN's definition of absolute poverty, which is the severe deprivation, or lack, of any two of seven basic needs: adequate food, safe drinking water, sanitation facilities, health care,

People who live in cold climates need different resources than those who live in warmer ones, including ways to stay warm in the winter.

adequate shelter, access to information, and access to education. For example, Gordon defined water deprivation as "access only to unimproved source such as open wells, open springs or surface water or who have to walk for more than 15 minutes to their water source (30 minutes round-trip)."[2] He defined water deprivation as severe if someone had "access only to surface water (e.g. rivers, ponds) for drinking or living in households where the nearest source of water was more than 15 minutes away—30 [minutes] round trip."[3] According to Gordon's assessment, someone who has access only to surface water and also has no access to any kind of news source—including newspapers, the internet, a phone, or a radio—is considered to be living in absolute poverty, since that person lacks two of the seven basic needs (adequate water and access to information). By qualifying and further defining basic needs, Gordon's definition accounts for the differences in the costs of those needs in various places.

POVERTY HURTS

"Well-being isn't just about our relationship with things, it's also about our relationships with each other. Poverty hurts, not just because it can leave you feeling hungry, cold and sick, but because it can also leave you feeling ignored, excluded and ashamed."
—Don Arthur, blogger

Don Arthur, "What if Adam Smith Was Right About Poverty?," Club Troppo, June 22, 2008, clubtroppo.com.au/2008/06/22/what-if-adam-smith-was-right-about-poverty/.

Location Matters

Most experts agree, however, that measures of absolute poverty are insufficient. Not only do basic needs differ from place to place, but cultural expectations differ, too. To account for these differences, experts generally measure relative poverty, which compares people with each other. Relative poverty measures account for the social ties that people have to others. In the wealthiest countries, the poor may not live in absolute poverty. They may have access to the basic necessities and may, in fact, live in relative comfort compared with those who live in poverty in other places.

While relative poverty satisfies the need for different measures in different places, it also tends to highlight the economic inequality that exists between people who live in the same country. This is because measures of absolute poverty are objective. Someone either lives above or below the line. Relative poverty, on the other hand, is subjective; it compares living standards. Someone may be poorer than someone else, but neither may live in absolute poverty. All the same, the consequences of inequality can be devastating. As the gap between the rich and the poor widens, crime increases, health and education suffer, and families are affected. Anup Shah, whose website Global Issues addresses many of these topics, explained, "Some of these things are hard to measure, such as … the level of trust and comfort people will have in interacting with one another in the society. Nonetheless, over the years, numerous studies have shown that sometimes the poor in wealthy countries can be unhappier or [find] it harder to cope than poor people in poorer countries."[4]

For example, almost every family in the United States owns at least one television. However, this appliance is rare in parts of the world where electricity is absent or unreliable. Therefore, a resident of the United States without a television might feel deprived, while someone in a less-developed country who lives in a region without electricity would not expect to own a television at all. Moreover, even many of the poorest families in the United States have easy access to clean water, which flows from taps and flushes toilets. Such easy access to clean water is unimaginable in many developing countries.

A cell phone may seem like a luxury item, but in the United States, not having access to a cell phone may make it hard to stay in touch with others, leaving someone feeling left out and deprived.

A Denial of Opportunities

In the ongoing attempt to clarify the definition and causes of poverty, the heads of all agencies within the UN signed this statement in June 1998:

Fundamentally, poverty is a denial of choices and op-portunities, a violation of human dignity. It means lack of basic capacity to participate effectively in society. It means not having enough to feed and [clothe] a family, not having a school or clinic to go to, not having the land on which to grow one's food or a job to earn one's living, not having access to credit. It means insecurity, power-lessness and exclusion of individuals, households and communities. It means susceptibility to violence, and it often implies living on marginal or fragile environments, without access to clean water or sanitation.[1]

1. Quoted in David Gordon, "Indicators of Poverty and Hunger," University of Bristol, December 12-14, 2005, p. 4. www.poverty.ac.uk/sites/default/files/indicators-of-poverty-and-hunger_UNpoverty.pdf.

Two hundred years ago, economist Adam Smith addressed the issue of inequality in his book *An Inquiry into the Nature and Causes of the Wealth of Nations*. He wrote, "A linen shirt, for example, is, strictly speaking, not a necessary of life. The Greeks and Romans lived, I suppose, very comfortably, though they had no linen. But in the present times, through the greater part of Europe, a creditable day laborer would be ashamed to appear in public without a linen shirt."[5] This example of inequality is widely cited by other economists and poverty experts to emphasize the issue of inequality and the ways it changes over time. Smith is also credited with highlighting the association of poverty with shame. Most experts agree that this connection accounts for many of the social problems associated with poverty.

A monument to Adam Smith, an influential economist who wrote about poverty, is shown here.

The Structure of a Society Matters

Amartya Sen, an Indian economist and Harvard professor, has spent his professional life investigating the roots of the inequality of poverty. Sen grew up in India in the 1940s in the midst of a serious famine. Sen's family and the families of his friends led normal lives, but every day he witnessed starving people begging for food in the streets. In fact, 3 million Indians died of hunger during the Bengal famine in 1943. Though he was a young boy, Sen was disturbed and puzzled by the fact that in the same place, some people starved while others had enough to eat. Seeking the reasons for this inequality became the focus of Sen's work, both as a student and later as an economics professor. His studies confirmed his early suspicion that famine, one serious consequence of poverty, generally affects only a small proportion of the population—typically no more than 5 percent. Moreover, the factor most responsible for who has food and who does not is not the availability

Amartya Sen won the Nobel Prize for Economics in 1998 for his work on poverty.

of food, but the form of a country's government. Governments that do not elect leaders in democratic elections often have little interest in protecting their most economically vulnerable citizens, Sen found. This finding held true in every country he studied, including China, the Soviet Union, and countries in sub-Saharan Africa.

When asked to explain, Sen said,

The first answer is that the government servants and the leaders are upper class. They never starve. They never suffer from famine, and therefore they don't have a personal incentive to stop it. However, if the government were vulnerable to public opinion, then famines are a dreadfully bad thing to have. You can't win many elections after a famine.[6]

Sen pointed out that poverty and its effects are a complex combination of political, social, and economic factors. Sen's best-known book, *Poverty and Famines: An Essay on Entitlement and Deprivation*, was published in 1981. He won the Nobel Prize for Economics in 1998 for his work on poverty and democracy. Decisions about foreign aid for developing countries are often based on Sen's work.

Creating Wealth

President Barack Obama and his family visited Ghana in summer 2009 on his first official visit to a country in sub-Saharan Africa. Crowds lined the street in the capital city of Accra to greet the first African American U.S. president. Obama's father was born in the African country of Kenya, and Obama has spoken of a special connection to the people of Africa. His message in Ghana was warm but stern. He cautioned that Ghana must monitor the honesty of its institutions and government. He said,

> No country is going to create wealth if its leaders exploit the economy to enrich themselves, or police can be bought off by drug traffickers ... No business wants to invest in a place where the government skims 20 percent off the top, or the head of the port authority is corrupt. No person wants to live in a society where the rule of law gives way to the rule of brutality and bribery. That is not democracy; that is tyranny, and now is the time for it to end. Africa doesn't need strongmen. It needs strong institutions.[1]

Obama's remarks emphasized the point that a dishonest government creates poverty for its citizens.

1. Quoted in Peter Baker, "Obama Delivers Call for Change to a Rapt Africa," *New York Times*, July 12, 2009. www.nytimes.com/2009/07/12/world/africa/12prexy.htm.

Coming Together

Regardless of whether poverty is discussed in absolute or relative terms, and despite the political issues involved, fighting poverty on a global scale requires cooperation. World governments, the UN, and other global institutions, as well as anti-poverty agencies, must work together to battle this universal problem. The most powerful weapon they have is shared understanding. To that end, countries are generally divided into economic categories. These categories are based on several factors, which include the income of people who live there, the rate of literacy, and how efficiently a country runs its business and industry.

The world's poorest countries are generally referred to as "developing countries" or the "Global South." In general, these countries have low rates of literacy; high rates of disease and malnutrition; lack of basic infrastructure such as roads, systems of communication, and energy; and poor living conditions. In many developing countries, powerful leaders make the major economic decisions and control the wealth. These leaders may not be interested in helping the poor. They may not have enough resources, or they may not know how to manage resources. People who live in developing countries may have little input into or influence with the government or economy of the place in which they live, so their needs are not a priority for the leaders or the government.

"Developed countries"—also referred to as the "Global North"—such as the United States and most of western Europe lie at the opposite end of the spectrum. In developed countries, democratically elected representatives make most of the important decisions. These representatives have more motivation to serve the people who elect them, both rich and poor. Business and industry is privately owned. Industries in developed countries generally operate with modern technology. Prices for products and wages for workers in developed countries are mostly determined by the market, not by the government or a strong leader. When products are plentiful, prices fall, and when supplies are limited, prices rise. Similarly, employment remains high when the economy is strong and falls if the economy weakens. This system is called capitalism.

While wealthy countries do have areas where housing is substandard and unemployment is high, the overall living standard is generally higher in developed countries than it is in developing countries. Almost everyone in the United States, for example, owns a phone and a television. They have food and access to a washer and dryer to clean their clothes. All U.S. children must attend school, and almost every adult citizen in the United States has the right to vote. This does not mean poor people in the United States do not struggle; it just means they have access to more resources than those in a developing country.

In a speech to the UN in 2000, Kofi Annan, who was secretary general of the UN at the time, distinguished between developed and developing countries. He said, "A developed country is one that allows all its citizens to enjoy a free and healthy life in a safe environment. And a genuinely developing country is one in which civil society is able to insist, not only on material well being, but on improving standards of human rights and environmental protection as well."[7] As of June 2017, the UN has named 47 countries in Africa, eastern Europe, and Asia as "least developed." These include Somalia, Haiti, Mozambique, Uganda, Yemen, Burundi, Djibouti, and Kiribati. The list of least developed countries (LDCs) is reviewed and updated every three years. The United States, Canada, Japan, Australia, New Zealand, Israel, South Africa, and most countries in western Europe are generally considered developed nations.

Many countries do not fall neatly into either the "developing" or the "developed" category. Some are undergoing rapid economic changes. These countries are said to be countries with "transitional economies." China, Vietnam, and many countries in eastern Europe that were once part of the Union of Soviet Socialist Republics (USSR) are among those countries that are in transition.

Poverty in Different Places

Poverty has different causes in different parts of the world, but the effects of extreme poverty are universally devastating. A majority of the world's poorest countries are found in Africa, though some African countries are poorer than others. South Africa and Egypt, for example, fare better than Angola and Ethiopia. While absolute poverty has decreased in some African nations, the poverty in many African countries relative to the rest of the world has actually increased.

Poverty in Africa has multiple causes. In many parts of Africa, farmers rely solely on rainfall for irrigation. Food production, therefore, has been devastated by ongoing periods of drought. Civil war in some African countries has created great economic hard-

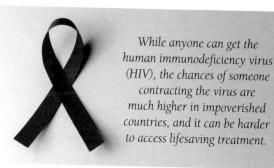

While anyone can get the human immunodeficiency virus (HIV), the chances of someone contracting the virus are much higher in impoverished countries, and it can be harder to access lifesaving treatment.

ship for many Africans; millions have been forced by war or other violent conflict to become refugees in neighboring countries. Others threatened by ethnic violence have lost their source of income. Lack of access to clean water in Africa results in the spread of diseases, which also complicates efforts to improve education and health care. The human immunodeficiency virus (HIV) and acquired immunodeficiency syndrome (AIDS) are widespread and serious problems that wreak havoc on many elements of African life.

Poverty in Latin America, like poverty in Africa, is widespread and more severe in some countries than others. The people who are native to those countries suffer most from poverty. In some regions, the land itself presents challenges. Rocky, mountainous terrain and climatic challenges such as extreme heat and cold make it difficult to transport products and build and maintain roads and energy plants. Millions of acres of rain forests in South and Central America are being cleared annually for short-term benefit, such as agriculture and products for wealthy countries, yet their destruction results in long-term devastation for peasant farmers who depend on rain forests for their lifestyle and resources. Population growth, migration, the drug trade, and political instability also add to ongoing poverty in Latin America.

Asia is home to the majority of the world's poorest people, mainly because Asia is home to the majority of the world's population overall. Though China has made remarkable progress in recent years and the economies of Japan and South Korea are growing, widespread poverty persists throughout the continent. South Asia (including parts of India, Bangladesh, and Nepal), Southeast Asia (including Cambodia, Laos, East Timor, and Myanmar), and even many regions in East Asia, including China's interior and North Korea, continue to suffer from extreme poverty. Disease, lack of education, hunger, and unsafe housing—all consequences of extreme poverty—afflict the people in these regions just as they do the impoverished populations in Africa, Latin America, and other parts of the world.

Poverty in Developed Nations

Populations in poor countries are not alone in their struggles with poverty. People live in poverty in some of the richest countries as well. Wealth is not distributed equally. According to the most recent statistics available from the United States Census Bureau, about 14.5 percent of Americans live below the poverty line. Within that percentage, some are poorer than others. In the United Kingdom (UK), the Office for National Statistics found that 33 percent of the population had been in poverty at least once in their lives, but only 7.8 percent lived in poverty consistently. This is better than the average for the European Union (EU), which is 15.9 percent. The poor in rich countries face just as many challenges as the poor in developing countries in overcoming their financial difficulties. However, not all of the challenges are the same. For instance, while it is often acknowledged that the poor in developing countries are impoverished through no fault of their own, in wealthy countries, the poor are often blamed for their financial difficulties, which makes it that much harder to find jobs and improve prospects. The cycle of poverty is difficult to stop anywhere in the world.

A study published in 2002 by leading world economist Branko Milanovic underscored the vast differences between the world's richest and poorest citizens. Milanovic studied 91 countries making up 85 percent of the world's population. He concluded that the richest 1 percent of people in the world earned as much as the poorest 57 percent put together. An article in a British newspaper highlighted the results of the study. It pointed out, "Four fifths of the world's population live below what countries in North America and Europe consider the poverty line. The poorest 10% of Americans are still better off than two-thirds of the world population."[8]

Those Left Behind

Some countries have managed to lower their poverty levels. World economists frequently cite China's dramatic success in raising its standard of living. The percentage of China's population that fell below the poverty line decreased from 88 percent in 1981 to only 6.5 percent in 2012. Educated people who live and work in China's big cities generally have plenty of food, comfortable shelter, and easy access to health care. They own cars, computers, cell phones, and other luxuries associated with a comfortable income. However, rural peasants do not fare as well. A *New York Times* article explained in 2008, "In village after village, people are too poor to heat their homes in the winter and many lack basic comforts like running water. Mobile phones, a near ubiquitous [almost everywhere] symbol of upward mobility throughout much of this country, are seen as an impossible luxury."[9] Though poverty rates were higher overall in the early 1980s, the lives of most Chinese citizens at that time closely resembled the lives of their neighbors. Now, Chinese society is sharply divided like the societies of many of the wealthiest nations.

While defining poverty may seem like a vocabulary exercise, anti-poverty programs use the statistics and definitions of poverty to drive their programs. Governments, politicians, and organizations that battle poverty use the numbers to suit their purposes. Each change in the definition of poverty, like each change in the poverty line, has repercussions. Likewise, the causes of poverty are also wide-ranging and not fully understood. Each cause has multiple effects; each effect becomes another cause. However, no matter how it is defined or why it is so widespread, one truth cannot be denied: In the 21st century, more than 3 billion people on the earth—more than half of the people in the world—struggle in poverty each day.

CHAPTER 2

The Complex Cycle of Poverty

For the experts who study poverty, it almost seems to take on a life of its own. There are ways to help the symptoms of poverty, of course. If someone is hungry, they can be given a hot meal. If someone does not have a place to live, a house can be built for them. If someone does not have access to clean water, people can bring in plumbers, drill wells, and set up a state-of-the-art running water infrastructure. However, treating the symptoms may not eliminate the condition of poverty. When the hot meal is gone, or the house is destroyed in a natural disaster, or a pipe bursts after the plumbers have left, the people who received this temporary help may find themselves back in the same situation they were in to begin with.

The root causes of poverty are complex, and there is debate about how exactly it all works. Most experts agree that there are many factors that can cause poverty, not just one. Where people live, whether the government in a country is stable, what resources are available, what sort of crops grow, where the nearest lake or river is, and societal injustice all play a role. Poverty is called a cycle because even if people fix one small part of the problem, it seems as if poverty will continue under its own momentum. For instance, the community water system that was built may break down because there are not enough resources to maintain it, there is nowhere for aspiring plumbers to go to school, or it is not possible to buy the right parts nearby; sooner or later, the people will have to go back to walking several miles to fetch water from a nearby stream, risking water-borne diseases in the process.

To fight poverty effectively, it is important to understand how this complex cycle works and all the pieces that need to be addressed to improve people's lives. It is not enough to just donate money to people if they do not have a way to use it to make lasting change. Organizations that fight poverty have to spend a lot of time thinking about how to tackle this complex and difficult problem.

A FAIR CHANCE

"Very often a lack of jobs and money is not the cause of poverty, but the symptom. The cause may lie deeper in our failure to give our fellow citizens a fair chance to develop their own capacities."
–Lyndon B. Johnson, 36th president of the United States from 1963 to 1969

"Lyndon B. Johnson, State of the Union address, January 8, 1964," USA Presidents, accessed December 19, 2017. www.usa-presidents.info/union/lbj-1.html.

Geographic Luck

Jared Diamond, a professor of geography at the University of California, Los Angeles, is one expert who has devoted his work to determining why people in some parts of the world thrive while others struggle. In his book *Guns, Germs, and Steel*, Diamond examined 10,000 years of human history and concluded that "geographic luck" is the key to success, disagreeing with those who believe poverty and wealth are determined by someone's natural intelligence, motivation, or creativity.

Diamond explained that certain wild plants grew in distinct regions in ancient times and were easier to cultivate and more nutritious than others. This led to the development of farming in some places. Plentiful harvests provided time for people to develop other skills. Civilizations with advanced skills gained power and expanded.

Some environments have more resources than others. For example, wheat cannot grow in the desert.

Diamond's work is filled with evidence of the intelligence, motivation, and creativity of people from cultures that have historically struggled. Since civilizations first blossomed, people's resourcefulness has been reflected in how they produced goods and traded with distant cultures. Until recently, trade was limited to products and crops. These goods, which are known as commodities, are manufactured or grown in one physical place and then shipped to another. However, trade has expanded. In the beginning of the 21st century, trade included services, money, and information—which have no physical roots—in addition to commodities. Everything moves with increasing ease among nations. The network that moves money and information is not a network of freighters, trucks, and trains, but a network powered by the internet.

The fluid movement of goods, services, and information among countries is called globalization. One outcome of globalization is the increasing competition between countries for valuable resources, including knowledge and ideas. Countries compete for talented workers; they compete for tourists; and they compete to have multinational businesses base headquarters in their cities. Each time one country outdoes another in this ongoing competition, the winner is rewarded with increased income and tax revenues. The losing country faces fewer jobs and increased poverty.

Advocates of globalization insist that it spreads the world's wealth. Critics argue that it hurts the poor. A book titled *Globalization and Poverty* published in 2007 by the National Bureau of Economic Research explored these issues and concluded that the poor benefit from globalization if they are part of a country's formal economy. They must have credit, the ability to travel to regions that employ workers, and the technical know-how to fulfill requirements of new jobs. However, there is also evidence that the poor suffer from globalization.

One example of this is the Olympic Games that happen every two years. Countries compete to be the host city by putting in a bid with the International Olympic Committee. Bids cost millions of dollars; according to Investopedia, "Cities typically spend $50 million to $100 million in fees for consultants, event organizers and travel related to hosting duties. For example, Tokyo lost approximately $150 million on its bid for the 2016 Olympics and spent approximately $75 million on its 2020 bid."[10] After the bid has been won, cities then spend millions more on things such as adding housing, improving roads and airports, and cleaning the city. Much of that money comes from taxpayers, which can put a strain even on those who are not poor.

Hosting the Olympics can have economic benefits for a city because the people who come to watch the games spend a lot of money there on hotels, food, and entertainment. Additionally, the improvements cities make often create new jobs and make life easier for citizens even after the Olympics are over. However, being the host city can also have significant drawbacks, and these disproportionately affect people who are already poor. For instance, when Salt Lake City, Utah, hosted the Winter Olympics in 2002, it "added only 7,000 jobs, about 10% of the number that officials had mentioned ... Also, most jobs went to workers who were already employed, which did not help the number of unemployed workers."[11] Most of the profits that came from people spending money in hotels and restaurants went to the international companies that owned those businesses, not to the host city. Additionally, most cities do not make enough in profit to justify the amount they spend on the bidding process and often actually end up in debt because of it. This means they have less money to spend on their citizens when the Olympics are over.

Most experts agree that globalization is responsible for increasing the inequality among people who live in the same country. New businesses and wealth that pour into metropolitan areas enrich the lives of city dwellers. However, people who live in rural villages do not get the same rewards. Their jobs are often threatened as new businesses and modern farms prosper, widening the gap between the rich and the poor.

The complexity of globalization contributes to the difficulty in assessing its effects. In a lecture titled "Globalization and the Fight Against Poverty," Robert I. Lerman, former director of the Urban Institute's Labor and Social Policy Center, explained that, in theory, globalization encourages growth, lowers poverty, and reduces inequality among countries. Lerman acknowledged the difficulty of pinpointing why some previously poor countries in Asia have prospered in response to globalization, while others—especially in Africa and Latin America—continue to struggle.

Lerman also noted that modern media has raised the world's awareness about poverty. He said, "More than ever, people can see or read about swollen stomachs of hungry African children, 11-year-old Asian children working in sweatshops, and Haitian families living in mud huts without medical care, electricity, or clean water. At the same time, many of the richest people are global celebrities."[12] Lerman cautioned, however, against confusing growing awareness of poverty with increasing incidence of poverty. Though the media focuses more attention on poverty than they once did, this increase in focus does not necessarily reflect accurately how poverty has changed. On the contrary, Lerman pointed to decreases in poverty in parts of China and India over the past two decades. He credits globalization with progress in those countries. In fact, although some places, such as Mexico, have seen an increase in poverty rates in the last several years, global poverty rates have reportedly been steadily decreasing. According to an April 17, 2013, press release by the World Bank,

> The number of people living on less than $1.25 per day has decreased dramatically in the past three decades, from half the citizens in the developing world in 1981 to 21 percent in 2010, despite a 59 percent increase in the developing world population. However, a new analysis of extreme poverty released today by the World Bank shows that there are still 1.2 billion people living in extreme poverty, and despite recent impressive progress, Sub-Saharan Africa still accounts for more than one-third of the world's extreme poor.[13]

Some have criticized announcements such as this because of how difficult it is to accurately calculate poverty statistics. These people have accused experts of overestimating the poverty decrease. In 2015, the World Bank announced that the percentage of people living in poverty around the world is at 9.6 percent—the first time it has been a single digit. This figure took into account the increase in the poverty line from $1.25 to $1.90. In response, *The Economist* published an article about the problems with this claim:

> The Bank bases its poverty figures on household surveys, which are undertaken by developing countries every few years. In the years between surveys, the Bank takes the last set of survey figures and shrinks them by assuming that the fortunes of the poor improve at the national growth rate. But the benefits of economic growth in many developing countries often [make the rich richer]. In India and China, inequality has been increasing in recent years. From 1981 to 2010, the average poor person in sub-Saharan Africa saw no increase in their income even as economies expanded. Because there is no household data since 2012, it is impossible to know if these trends toward greater inequality have since changed.[14]

Lerman admitted the topic of globalization and poverty is complex and multifaceted. However, he concluded, "it is time for opponents and proponents of globalization to join forces to help low-income countries expand their access to rich country markets and develop and nurture their governing institutions so that the world's poor gain from the benefits of a more integrated world."[15]

Percent of Population Living on Under $2 per Day

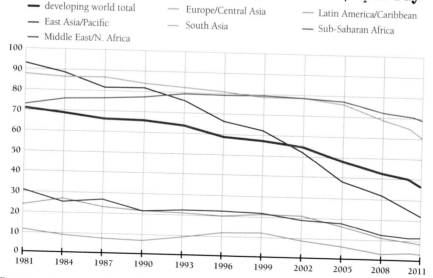

- developing world total
- East Asia/Pacific
- Middle East/N. Africa
- Europe/Central Asia
- South Asia
- Latin America/Caribbean
- Sub-Saharan Africa

Poverty rates around the world appear to have been decreasing steadily since the 1980s, as this information from Business Insider shows. However, some people believe these statistics may not be completely accurate.

THE IMPACT OF FAMINE

"[Too] many developing countries have neglected investment in agriculture, leading to starvation and malnutrition. Hungry people are desperate people, and periodic famines and food shortages can cause mass migrations that disrupt entire regions."
—Richard Lugar, former U.S. senator from Indiana

"Lugar Encourages Obama to Focus on Food, Energy, Corruption," U.S. Senate, July 10, 2009. lugar.senate.gov/press/record.cfm?id=315621&&

Outsourcing

One outcome of globalization is the movement of American manufacturing centers to cities overseas. Workers in many developing countries are willing to work for less money than American workers. When an American company, such as an automobile manufacturer, moves its factories to a foreign city and hires workers there to make its products, it is said to be outsourcing its labor force. This significant shift in location of jobs is demonstrated when American customers call a company's billing department or product support line and increasingly find themselves connected to a service center in India. Workers there learn to speak English with neutral, non-regional accents and adopt American names to increase customer satisfaction.

Outsourcing is a complicated topic that has benefits as well as drawbacks. Some say outsourcing is bad for the U.S. economy because each job that is outsourced involves the loss of a job in the home country and the addition of a job overseas, contributing to increased poverty in the home country. Some also say outsourcing is bad for the workers in the developing countries who receive the jobs. This is because in the United States and other developed countries that outsource jobs, strict laws govern wages and benefits, manufacturing quality, and the safety of workers. In other parts of the world, however, the pressure to produce goods quickly and cheaply often results in less oversight and the exploitation, or unfair treatment, of workers. Outsourcing can mean substandard working conditions, child labor, and low wages. According to DoSomething.org, "In developing countries, an estimated 168 million children ages 5 to 14 are forced to work."[16] In addition to these ethical problems, outsourcing often produces goods that are of poor quality, especially in the case of clothing. Because they are cheaper to produce in other countries, the prices are lower when they are sold in the United States, but they often wear out more quickly. People who buy cheap items to save money may not actually be saving money in the long term.

People who support outsourcing say it creates jobs overseas and helps reduce poverty in developing nations. They also say the jobs that are outsourced are ones American citizens would prefer not to do, which allows companies to increase productivity and open up higher-paying jobs in the United States, although this would only benefit higher-skilled workers; lower-skilled workers, who are often poorer, would lose rather than gain jobs. Additionally, they say that although people in the overseas country are making less money than an American would, it is still more than they would be making in other jobs their home country offers. Opponents counter this by saying that wages should be absolute, not relative. They point out that the overseas workers generally have to work much longer hours in worse conditions to make less money than an American would for the same job and that when working conditions endanger a person's health, the amount of money they are making is not important.

Many companies continue to outsource their customer service due to cheaper costs.

Outsourcing is a hotly debated topic and was a major point in the 2016 U.S. presidential campaign, when both candidates promised to increase the number of jobs available in the United States and criticized certain companies for sending jobs overseas. This debate will likely continue for years, and it is made more complicated by the fact that accurate data is hard to find. As journalist Lydia DePillis wrote in the *Washington Post*, "It's very difficult to get a handle on how many jobs have been lost due to outsourcing, and how many might have been created in the U.S. as a result."[17] Even policy experts who have studied economics for years sometimes disagree on whether outsourcing is good or bad for countries' economies and citizens.

Access to Electricity

Many developing countries suffer from "energy poverty," a term used by Robert Freling, executive director of the Solar Electric Light Fund (SELF). SELF delivers solar power and wireless communications to rural villages throughout the world. About 16 percent of the world's population—1.2 billion people—lacks regular access to electricity.

The lack of energy has powerful consequences. According to Freling, "At the village level, energy poverty means you can't pump water regularly, there's no communications, no way to have adult literacy classes, and certainly no way to run computers at school. Energy poverty creeps into every single aspect of existence and wipes out any hope of climbing out of [economic] poverty into the twenty-first century."[18] Countries that do not have consistent energy cannot benefit from the lightning-speed communications they need to contribute to and benefit from the growing interconnectedness of the world's economy. They are left out of the exchange of ideas and resources that take place among countries that are plugged in to the global marketplace. Many places with widespread energy poverty have certain places where people can access the internet, such as a library or school. However, the connection is often slow, there are generally many people waiting to take a turn on the computer, and they may have to walk far to get there, which means they cannot use it regularly. Additionally, while individual internet access can improve quality of life by increasing communication and access to information, it does not generally contribute to a country's overall economic growth.

Energy poverty is the result of many factors. In some regions, rapid population growth overwhelms available energy supplies. In others, the high cost of oil and gas limits access to energy. Droughts undermine hydroelectric power plants that require fast-flowing rivers and full dams to operate. Corruption, or dishonest actions by people in power, is widespread in many developing countries, which results in government money spent on things that benefit a few select people rather than the majority of the population. Countries that suffer from corruption or ongoing civil wars, such as those in parts of Asia and Africa, do not function well enough to manage expensive, complex energy grids.

Access to electricity can significantly increase quality of life, but there are many people in the world who cannot simply flip on a light switch when it gets dark at night.

The Role of Government Corruption

Corruption is blamed for more than energy shortages. In fact, corruption is blamed for much of the ongoing poverty in developing countries. Human Rights Watch pointed to the dictatorship of President Teodoro Obiang Nguema Mbasogo of Equatorial Guinea, Africa, as a prime example. The dictator mishandled billions of dollars in oil revenue. Since vast fields of oil were discovered there in the 1990s, the country's financial resources surged more than 5000 percent. The country is now the third-largest oil producer in sub-Saharan Africa. However, 70 percent of Equatorial Guinea's 700,000 people still live in extreme poverty. Between 2004 and 2006, the dictator's son spent

$43.5 million on a lavish lifestyle, which is more than the government spent the same year on education. Arvind Ganesan of Human Rights Watch explained, "Here is a country where people should have the per capita wealth of Spain or Italy, but instead they live in conditions comparable to Chad or the Democratic Republic of the Congo ... This is a testament to the government's corruption, mismanagement, and callousness [heartlessness] toward its own people."[19]

HEALTH MATTERS

"You cannot drive economic growth in a place where 50 percent of the people are infected with malaria or half of the kids are malnourished or a third of the mothers are dying of AIDS."
—Thomas L. Friedman, American journalist and author

Thomas L. Friedman, *The World Is Flat.* New York, NY: Farrar, Straus & Giroux, 2005, p. 378.

Corruption is not limited to African countries. A 2008 report by Transparency International (TI), a Canadian human rights group, reported that corruption is global and contributes to ongoing poverty and inequality between the rich and the poor. In the 2016 version of a yearly report titled "Corruption Perceptions Index 2016," TI ranked 176 countries from 0 (very corrupt) to 100 (very clean). It noted that although some countries did better than others, more than two-thirds scored below 50, and the global average was 43. Denmark, New Zealand, Finland, and Sweden received top scores, while Somalia, South Sudan, and North Korea ranked at the bottom. The United States scored 74 and ranked 18th; it had been steadily improving until that point, but the 2016 score represents a two-point drop from the 2015 score.

TI chairman Huguette Labelle sees a direct link between corruption and poverty. She explained,

If you are in a country with a lot of natural resources, with a lot of money moving into the government, but that money is being diverted [to government officials] ... instead of going in for the

development of a country, that does mean that the school will not be built, the health system will not be there, and the infrastructure will be weak, so that we will have poverty as a result.[20]

She pointed out that wealthy countries are also at risk for corruption, citing "the continuing emergence of foreign bribery scandals."[21] She believes conditions of aid should include built-in systems that ensure transparency (allowing nothing to be hidden), and donations from foreign countries or organizations should target projects that a country really needs or wants.

A Vicious Cycle

When people talk about the cycle of poverty, they mean that people who are disadvantaged often stay disadvantaged and pass that disadvantage on to their children. Starting out disadvantaged means those children stay disadvantaged and pass it on to their own children, and it continues that way until something happens to break the cycle. Unfortunately, this is incredibly hard to do, and there are many different factors that keep it going in the United States.

One example of the cycle of poverty is Lori Lebo from Reading, Pennsylvania, who was 37 in 2012, when National Public Radio (NPR) interviewed her. She had an abusive boyfriend and their daughter, Mikaela, was born prematurely. This meant she needed a lot of medical care and Lebo had to stay home with her a lot. She was fired from her job for missing too much work to stay home with her daughter and go to court after her boyfriend broke her nose. Losing her job then made it harder to pay for childcare; she was getting financial assistance from the government to pay for it, but those benefits only go to people who have jobs. Since she could not afford daycare or a babysitter for Mikaela and her other child, Jeffrey, who was nine years old at that time, Lebo had difficulty going to interviews to find another job. All of these conditions contributed to keeping Lebo and her family in poverty, putting Mikaela and Jeffrey at a disadvantage for the future—for instance, as they get older, Lebo may not have enough money to send them to college, which will limit their job prospects.

Leaving Home to Escape Poverty

Poverty creates corruption and corruption creates poverty. Immigration acts in the same way. People uproot themselves and move to a new place hoping to escape poverty, only to find their move adds to the misery they hoped to leave behind. They may face an unfamiliar language and new customs, rules that limit job and educational opportunities, and a lack of extended family support.

The reasons for immigration are commonly referred to as "push and pull factors." People are "pulled" from their homelands by the hope of a better job, family ties, or an education. They believe they will find better opportunities in the United States, England, France, Australia, and other developed nations. Other times, people are "pushed" from their homelands by civil wars and desperate poverty.

Reporter Sonia Nazario won a Pulitzer Prize for her book *Enrique's Journey*, an account of the stressful journey of one teenage boy from Honduras to the United States in search of his mother. Enrique's mother left him in the care of his grandmother when he was five and immigrated to the United States to find work. This was the only way she felt she could provide for him, Nazario explained. *Enrique's Journey* is both a terrifying tale of his journey and a critique of U.S. immigration policy. Nazario claimed that "politicians have put a lock on the front door while swinging the back door wide open."[22] She explained that while polls show that Americans want to crack down on undocumented immigration, businesses such as agriculture, construction, food processing, restaurants, and domestic help agencies depend on cheap immigrant labor to operate at a profit. The result is that undocumented immigrants who cross into the United States hoping to escape the poverty in their home countries are often exploited and remain in poverty while contributing to the overall wealth of their new country.

This attitude toward immigration is one that many people find difficult to reconcile with their own backgrounds. Except for those whose ancestors are Native Americans, everyone in the United States is descended from immigrants or people who were brought to the country against their will as slaves. This fuels a conflict about the justice of closing the door to new immigrants to reduce poverty rates. The United States, in particular, takes pride in its heritage as a land of opportunity, where anyone can succeed if he or she is willing to work hard.

Poverty in the United States

Although immigration can contribute to living in poverty, many people who have been U.S. citizens for generations live below the poverty line. There are many complex reasons for this, and often, they are interconnected.

Race is a major factor in determining who lives in poverty in the United States. Data from the United States Census shows that as of 2015, 24.1 percent of black people and 21.4 percent of Latinx live in poverty. Asians and whites have comparatively low rates of poverty, at 11.4 percent and 9 percent, respectively. However, this data—along with much of the news media—ignores Native Americans, who are known to have high rates of poverty. According to the Pew Research Center, in 2012, the Native American poverty rate was 29.1 percent, although it is higher on many reservations; for instance, on the Standing Rock

The inscription on the Statue of Liberty includes "bring me your poor," a reflection of the fact that poverty can drive people to leave their homes and immigrate to the United States.

Reservation, which is between North Dakota and South Dakota, the poverty rate is 43.2 percent. Although it is frequently stated that black people have the highest rate of poverty of any race, it is actually Native Americans who do.

The reason why race plays such an important role has to do with the historical treatment of these races. For instance, many black people are the descendants of slaves. Their families started out with nothing, and even after slavery ended, policies were put in place to ensure that they stayed poor—for instance, Jim Crow laws, which governed segregation and were in effect from 1877 to the 1950s. Segregation was supposed to be about "separate but equal" facilities; for instance, there were all-black schools and all-white schools, supposedly with the same advantages. However, in practice, the all-black schools were given outdated textbooks and fewer materials and resources, which put black students at a disadvantage compared with their white peers. Although segregation has ended, inner-city schools with primarily black students as well as schools on Native American reservations face many of the same problems. While Native Americans were not generally kept as slaves, they had their land and possessions stolen by settlers and later by the American government. Although reservations are technically part of the United States, they do not receive the same resources, advantages, and economic opportunities as other parts of the country. Even those who do not live on reservations may be poor due to the cycle of poverty. Because they are rarely mentioned in the news, most people have no idea how much of a problem poverty is for many Native Americans.

Although segregation is not an official government policy anymore, racist attitudes persist, even when people are not aware of them. Additionally, negative attitudes toward people who live in poverty contribute to keeping those people in poverty. For instance, many people believe someone who has a cell phone or new clothes cannot be poor. This attitude overlooks several facts. First of all, circumstances can change very quickly, and the person may have had that item while they still lived above the poverty line. For instance, someone may get sick and end up with large hospital bills, especially if they are not able to afford good health insurance. This can be the start of the cycle of poverty for them, and it can move fast, especially if another crisis hits at the same time—for example, if someone who is already struggling to pay off bills loses their job.

Additionally, although some people think a person's money would be better spent on something other than a phone contract, a cell phone is often a necessary item. Without one, it is difficult for prospective employers to contact a job seeker, for someone to call their bank and discuss their finances, or for someone to keep in touch with friends and family who may be able to provide support.

Having a strong support network is important for a variety of reasons. They can provide emotional support, potentially stopping someone from turning to drugs or alcohol when their circumstances make them feel sad, scared, or angry; although these substances provide a temporary escape from reality, an addiction makes life in poverty even harder than it already is, especially when someone starts spending a lot of money on it. A support network can also provide services the person might not otherwise be able to afford. For example, childcare is expensive, so having a relative who is able to babysit for free can be extremely helpful. When people have no support system to rely on, it contributes to keeping them in poverty.

Another factor that makes it hard to break out of poverty is the difficulty of saving money on a low income. Some people work several jobs yet still make very little money. Most of their paycheck must go to necessary things such as rent, food, and clothing. If there is any left after that, it can go into savings, but it takes time to build up a savings account. If a large expense happens unexpectedly, such as a trip to the hospital or important repairs to the house, it can wipe out a person's savings, and they will have to start all over again. Without savings to fall back on, it is difficult for someone to buy things that would improve their circumstances, such as a nice suit for a job interview or a house in a better neighborhood.

Many people do not realize how much poverty is influenced by where a person lives. Most people who are poor live in unsafe neighborhoods, which may make them the target of theft. The schools near these neighborhoods are often underfunded, which means the students do not have as many advantages as children who live in better neighborhoods, so they may have more difficulty getting into college and winning scholarships to pay for it. Students who come from wealthier families often do not need to rely on scholarships because their parents are able to help them pay for college, but impoverished students generally do not have that option. Loans are available to help people pay for school, but student debt typically takes years to pay off. The longer it takes, the more the interest—a penalty for not paying back debt quickly enough—adds up, which keeps someone in debt no matter how much they pay off. Because of this problem with loans, some students choose not to take them out, but then they may have no way to pay for college. Without a college education, their job prospects are limited. Jobs are also influenced by a person's location. Many people who live in poverty do not own cars and rely on walking or public transportation. If public transportation in their area is not good, it may not be a reliable option for them to get to work; for example, it may take someone in a major city up to two hours to get across town on the bus or subway. If the public transportation is often late, the person may be fired for not arriving to work on time, even though it is not their fault. If they try to get around this problem by only working at places that are within walking distance, they may find that they are unable to get a job that pays better than minimum wage.

The causes of poverty are complex, far reaching, and interconnected; these are only a few of the dozens of complex factors that contribute to keeping someone in poverty once they have fallen into it. Others include poor education about how to control finances, the difficulty of getting government aid, the social stigma (negative view) that comes with being poor, the effect of mental illness and the difficulty of affording treatment for it, and the fact that many companies no longer give raises to employees who have worked there for a long time. These problems may stack on top of each other, causing something called compounded poverty. Poverty does not just mean not having a lot of money; it can also relate to access to housing, education, employment, and health care. According to *The Atlantic*, which reported on a study published by a research group called the Brookings Institution,

> [T]he majority of blacks and Hispanics live with at least one form of poverty, while the majority of whites do not. And for white Americans who do experience one form of poverty, it's pretty unlikely that they experience any others. For instance, if both a white and black

American have low incomes, the white American is more likely to live in a better neighborhood, in better housing, and to have better access to superior education and healthcare ...

The findings [of the report] also illuminate why poverty can be so difficult to escape. The Brookings researchers note that anti-poverty solutions often focus on solving only one problem at a time—usually income, because it's the most pervasive and, perhaps, the easiest to quantify. They argue that in order to address the compounding effects of the various types of poverty, it would actually be useful to de-emphasize the matter of income. That may sound counterproductive, but it would just mean working to offer things like better quality public education, low-cost, comprehensive health care, and safer, higher-quality affordable housing, things that could improve the lives of all Americans, regardless of income limitations.[23]

The effort to understand poverty and break its destructive cycle is intense and ongoing. Each time one cause is identified and a strategy is worked out to counter that cause, poverty arises in a new form with equally devastating consequences. The battle against poverty requires an equally strategic and interconnected plan.

CHAPTER 3

What Can Be Done About Poverty?

While poverty is generally never considered a good thing—the suffering it causes is undeniable—people can and do disagree wildly about what should be done about it. Part of this is because it is such a complex problem. There is a lot of debate as to the causes of poverty, but the people who are living in poverty today do not have time to wait until that debate is settled. In the meantime, society has to fight poverty with whatever imperfect solutions it can come up with.

Much of the debate about how to fight poverty comes down to direction: bottom up or top down. Some experts think wealthier people and countries should donate their wealth to initiatives that help the poor. They believe the way to get rid of poverty is for those at the top to hand money and resources down to those living in poverty. Other experts disagree, however. These experts believe in a bottom up approach: Investors and businesses should help those living in poverty start businesses, grow in-demand crops, and work their way up from poverty, and governments should play a limited role. Many non-governmental organizations (NGOs) that fight poverty try to take a middle ground: Some of their funding comes from government grants, and they also work with individuals and businesses on the ground. No matter which approach someone favors, the intention is the same—to pull people out of poverty.

The Great Society

The first half of the 1960s was an eventful era in the United States. In May 1961, the first American blasted into space. Two years later, President John F. Kennedy was assassinated. Following constitutional procedure, Vice President Lyndon Baines Johnson took the oath of office within hours of Kennedy's death. Johnson inherited the escalating Vietnam War and ongoing tension between the Soviet Union and the United States. As he campaigned for election the following year, Johnson launched a vision for America that he called the Great Society. Johnson claimed the Great Society would be a place "where no child will go unfed and no youngster will go unschooled; where every child has a good teacher and every teacher has good pay, and both have good classrooms; where every human being has dignity and every worker has a job."[24]

To realize his vision, Johnson committed his new administration to a "war on poverty." To wage this war, he urged Congress to expand the role of the federal government to help the poor. Congress passed bills that raised the minimum wage and set up the Department of Housing and Urban Development to protect tenants and control rents. The government enacted a college loan system for poor students. Medicaid and Medicare helped pay for health care for the poor and elderly. By the time Johnson left office in 1969, the number of social programs in the country had

Lyndon B. Johnson was committed to a "war on poverty."

increased from 45 to 435. The poverty rate in the country fell during the Johnson administration from 19 percent in 1964 to 12.2 percent in 1969. This newly active role played by the U.S. government also changed expectations. People came to depend on the federal government to ensure adequate health care, housing, education, income, and employment. They accepted Johnson's notion that it was the government's responsibility to provide these services to those unable to do so. Conservative critics, however, believed then and continue to insist that social programs developed and paid for by the government actually harm the country by draining resources and making the poor dependent on the government instead of helping themselves.

People who support this view sometimes believe people are poor because they are lazy, which means they ignore many of the problems that contribute to long-term poverty. Ignoring the problems means they cannot be solved. Additionally, it creates a stigma around people seeking help, which makes some people reluctant to do so. Someone may be eligible for a program such as food stamps but choose not to sign up for it because they are afraid of the negative reactions they may get. Since welfare programs are paid for with citizens' tax dollars, some people mistakenly believe this gives them a say in how people who receive welfare spend their money. For example, someone who receives food stamps may find the people in line behind them at the store studying their purchases and possibly even making comments about whether they should be allowed to buy certain things. When people are too nervous to seek government help their own taxes have contributed to, it is much harder for them to climb out of poverty.

A RICH NATION THAT DOES NOT SUPPORT ITS POOR

"By many standards—from health to education to environment—the US is far behind other rich countries, and Congress is poised to exacerbate [increase] existing inequality with a new tax bill that rewards the wealthy and helps them keep profits within the family."—Annalisa Merelli, journalist

Annalisa Merelli, "The UN Sent an Envoy to Investigate Extreme Poverty in the United States." Quartz, December 7, 2017. qz.com/1150167the-united-nations-is-investigating-poverty-in-alabama-and-other-states/.

Sustainable Development Goals

While the United States struggles with poverty at home, it is helping end poverty in developing countries as a member country of the UN. In 2015, the 193 member countries of the UN signed a plan titled "Sustainable Development Goals." These

17 goals described a global strategy for combating poverty. The Sustainable Development Goals (SDGs) replaced the Millennium Development Goals, which had intended to end poverty by 2015. The new plan outlines a variety of goals and measures to end poverty by 2030. The SDGs outnumber those in the earlier plan and are extremely ambitious. They are:

GOAL 1: No Poverty
GOAL 2: Zero Hunger
GOAL 3: Good Health and Well-being
GOAL 4: Quality Education
GOAL 5: Gender Equality
GOAL 6: Clean Water and Sanitation
GOAL 7: Affordable and Clean Energy
GOAL 8: Decent Work and Economic Growth
GOAL 9: Industry, Innovation and Infrastructure
GOAL 10: Reduced Inequality
GOAL 11: Sustainable Cities and Communities
GOAL 12: Responsible Production and Consumption
GOAL 13: Climate Action
GOAL 14: Life Below Water
GOAL 15: Life on Land
GOAL 16: Peace and Justice Strong Institutions
GOAL 17: Partnerships to achieve the Goal[25]

The Sustainable Development Goals were adopted by the UN in 2015.

The First Three Goals

The first goal to eliminate poverty is very straightforward and leaves no doubt as to its intention. However, it is not a simple thing to achieve. As has been shown, poverty is a complex and difficult problem, and it is affected by many factors. This goal is based on the figure of $1.90 per day. To consider this goal achieved, everyone in the world would need to have more than that amount to be able to meet their basic needs.

The second goal of eliminating hunger is similarly straightforward and challenging to achieve. Not only does this goal seek to make sure everyone in the world has enough food to eat, it seeks to end malnutrition as well. It is not enough to have just enough food to not starve; everyone should be able to eat a nutritious and well-balanced diet that includes all the vitamins and minerals their bodies need to be healthy. Rather than just having some bread to get them through the day, this goal demands a balance of healthy grains, fruits, and vegetables—and enough of them as well.

The third goal of health and well-being follows naturally from these. This goal hopes to eliminate the public health concerns that stem from poverty. It intends to reduce the spread of contagious diseases, such as HIV, malaria, and tuberculosis, which are much more common in impoverished parts of the world. Achieving this goal would mean everyone would have access to and be able to afford the medicine and health care they need. Furthermore, it would reduce infant mortality, or the number of children who die before reaching the age of five, as well as reducing maternal mortality, or the number of women who die while giving birth. High infant and maternal mortality rates are also associated with poverty. Finally, this goal also seeks to address other common public health concerns in impoverished communities to cut back on preventable deaths from accidents, hazardous working conditions, pollution, and substance abuse.

These three goals are nothing if not ambitious. They do not seek to simply make things a little bit better. They are not about making people's lives okay or achieving a bare minimum. Instead, the aim of these goals is for every person on earth to have a "good" life filled with enough money, food, and health to achieve their dreams. How can this be possible, with the complex tangle of problems that constitutes poverty? Fortunately, the goals that follow all contribute to these first goals.

The Goals Build on Each Other

The 14 goals that follow the first 3 are meant to address some of the complex factors that lead to poverty and keep people and communities trapped in its cycle. To escape poverty, people need education and resources. This is repeated on the website of the Global Campaign for Education (GCE), a grassroots movement whose goal is to end the global education crisis. According to the GCE, "No country has ever achieved continuous and rapid economic growth without first having at least 40% of its adults able to read and write."[26] The GCE also pointed out that a child born to a literate mother is 50 percent more likely to survive past the age of five. Universal education is also considered crucial in the fight against HIV/AIDS and malaria.

The fifth goal of promoting equality between men and women and empowering women may not seem related at first,

Education is crucial in the fight against poverty.

but studies confirm that when women and men share equally in making family decisions, more household resources are devoted to children. The empowerment of women within the family leads to stronger communities. Schools improve, and literacy rises. The United Nations Population Fund underscored the importance of this goal on its website: "Gender equality is acknowledged as being a key to achieving the other ... goals."[27]

The Importance of Sanitation

Goal six addresses the issue of safe drinking water and sanitation. Though AIDS and malaria claim millions of lives each year, diarrhea is the most deadly health concern of all, and unclean drinking water and other unsanitary conditions play a big part in causing diarrhea. According to UNICEF, a global group that supports education, equality, and research for children, more than 1,200 children die each day from the effects of diarrhea. In the United States, clean water often comes out of a faucet, but in one-sixth of the world, plumbing is rare. In many countries, women and children spend hours each day fetching clean water and carrying it back to their families. According to a study by United Nations University, ensuring safe drinking water and sanitation is the fastest way to eliminate poverty and improve health worldwide. Water is basic to development. Without clean drinking water, people do not stay healthy. Without health, they do not have the physical strength to grow food, go to school, build solid housing and community infrastructure, or maintain jobs. The university issued a statement claiming, "Simply installing toilets where needed throughout the world and ensuring safe water supplies would do more to end crippling poverty and improve world health than any other measure."[28]

SDGS CRITICIZED DUE TO COST

"Developing countries seem to think that the more goals there are, the more aid money they will receive. They are wrong. The SDGs are unfeasibly expensive. Meeting them would cost $2 trillion-3 trillion a year of public and private money over 15 years. That is roughly 15% of annual global savings, or 4% of world GDP. At the moment, Western governments promise to provide 0.7% of GDP in aid, and in fact stump up only about a third of that. Planning to spend many times the amount that countries fail to give today is pure fantasy." —*The Economist*

"The 169 Commandments," *The Economist*, March 26, 2015. www.economist.com/news/leaders/21647286-proposed-sustainable-development-goals-would-be-worse-useless-169-commandments.

Although many in the United States would agree that people in developing countries should have access to clean water, many do not realize there are places in their own country that have the same problem. Since 2014, the residents of Flint, Michigan, have not had clean water running through their taps. That year, to save money, the city switched its water supply from Lake

Huron to the local Flint River. However, after the switch was made, people started getting sick. The water was brown and smelled bad, so few people wanted to drink it; showering in it led to rashes and hair loss. Tests found dangerously high levels of iron and lead in the water caused by the water breaking down the pipes.

At first, government officials denied there was a problem. They claimed the water was safe and that switching the water source again would be too expensive. Eventually, after many more tests that proved there were unsafe chemicals in the water, the city was forced to switch water sources, and government officials were accused of covering up the fact that the water was dangerous so they could save money. However, the water still runs through the corroded pipes, so it is undrinkable by the time it comes out of the tap. Most people in Flint use bottled water to drink, cook, and shower with, but this is much more expensive for them than using tap water would be; additionally, they are still expected to pay their water bill even though the water is unusable. Some families pay as much as $160 per month. Government assistance has been slow in coming; about 20,000 pipes need to be replaced at an estimated cost of $500 million, and Fox News reported that figuring out "which pipes need to be replaced and where they're located has been a nightmare process because city records are written in pencil on index cards. Some cards dating back more than 50 years are no longer accurate."[29] Many Flint residents, as well as others who have been

following the story, believe the process is moving more slowly because Flint is one of the poorest cities in the United States. When other places deal with similar crises or with natural disasters, help often comes much more quickly, partially because they receive

People in Flint, Michigan, use bottled water.

much more media attention. Although news outlets have covered the Flint water crisis, the story is often quickly dropped and picked back up months or years later, leading most of the United States to believe the problem has already been resolved. Rather than sending aid to Flint, some people have told those who live there to simply move to another city—ignoring the fact that moving is a difficult and expensive process. The situation in Flint shows how poverty changes the way people respond to those who need help and creates disadvantages that only grow worse when a crisis occurs.

AN UNACCEPTABLE CONDITION

"More than 1 billion people still live in deep poverty, a state of affairs that is morally unacceptable given the resources and technology we have available today."
—World Bank

"Ending Extreme Poverty and Promoting Shared Prosperity." World Bank, April 19, 2013. go.worldbank. org/DM4A38OWJ0.

Life Below Water and on Land

The SDGs recognize the importance of the oceans in fighting poverty. More than 70 percent of the earth's surface is covered in water, and the oceans play a crucial role in fighting climate change. In fact, the ocean absorbs nearly one-third of carbon dioxide produced by humans. Furthermore, many people live along the ocean's coasts and depend on it to make a living. The ocean provides a source of food in protein-rich fish, and beautiful shorelines attract tourists, providing an economic boost to the communities that live there. To achieve the rest of the SDGs, the oceans must be protected. However, pollution seriously threatens the health of the oceans. That is why the SDGs include the goal of protecting life below water.

The oceans are not the only part of the planet threatened by environmental concerns; life on land is precarious as well. Climate change and warming global temperatures cause problems such as desertification, which is the expansion of unlivable desert terrain into areas that once were home to more wildlife and bodies of water. An increase in natural disasters, including hurricanes and flooding, can also make areas unlivable and reduce the amount of territory available to people and animals. This goal aims to protect biodiversity, or a healthy variety of

Keeping the oceans healthy can help improve the lives of those who live along or visit the coasts.

plants and animals living in a place, by trying to conserve endangered species. This goal will ensure that people's communities will remain places where they can live and flourish.

What Is Plumpy'Nut?

Every year, 3 million children die from malnutrition. However, the Nobel Prize-winning relief group Doctors Without Borders has developed a simple lifesaving food. Called Plumpy'Nut, it is a paste made from peanut butter, powdered milk, and powdered sugar and enriched with vitamins and minerals. It is squeezed out of a tube like toothpaste and does not require refrigeration or water, even after it has been opened. It can be given to anyone, even children in the most advanced stages of malnutrition who might get sick if they tried to eat other food. Additionally, it is a treatment that does not have to be given in a hospital, and it is very cheap to make and distribute. Milton Tectonidis, the chief nutritionist for Doctors Without Borders, explained the impact of Plumpy'Nut: "It's a revolution in nutritional affairs ... Now we have something. It is like an essential medicine. In three weeks, we can cure a kid that ... [looks] like they're half dead ... It's just, boom! It's a spectacular response."[1] Experts have said Plumpy'Nut "may just be the most important advance ever"[2] in the fight against child hunger.

1.   Quoted in Anderson Cooper, "A Lifesaver Called 'Plumpynut,'" *60 Minutes*, June 22, 2008. www.cbsnews.com/stories/2007/10/19/60minutes/main3386661.shtml?tag=contentMain;contentBody.

2.   Quoted in Sarah Morrison, "Plumpy'Nut: The Lifesaver That Costs ... Well, Peanuts," *Independent*, August 24, 2013. www.independent.co.uk/news/world/africa/plumpynut-the-lifesaver-that-costs-well-peanuts-8783650.html.

The Importance of Cooperation

The final SDG is less about achieving an end to poverty and more about the way to achieve it. This goal of partnering to achieve the other goals points out the importance of everyone working together to achieve a better life for those currently living in poverty. Not only must the countries of the world work together through organizations such as the UN, but partnerships must be forged between agencies, NGOs, and grassroots organizations. According to the UN's website,

> A successful sustainable development agenda requires partnerships between governments, the private sector and civil society. These inclusive partnerships built upon principles and values, a shared vision, and shared goals that place people and the planet at the centre, are needed at the global, regional, national and local level.[30]

Development Aid and Direct Aid

Foreign aid is central to discussions about reducing world poverty. There are many forms of foreign aid. Aid is generally categorized as development aid or direct aid. Development aid is money provided for long-term improvement of basic institutions, such as agriculture, health care, water delivery, or energy systems. Direct aid focuses on more immediate solutions to particular problems. Direct aid can be project aid, which targets a specific project, such as money to build a school or hospital. Food aid, another form of direct aid, is generally sent to a country following a natural disaster, such as an earthquake or drought. Food aid may be sent to a war-torn region to help feed displaced refugees. Technical assistance entails sending people who have special skills, such as doctors and engineers, to developing countries. Technical assistance might benefit long-term development or short-term projects.

Investment is another form of aid that can benefit long-term development or short-term projects. Groups of investors offer financial assistance to businesses. If the business is successful, the investors share in its profits. Investments in mining and agriculture, for example, are important to economies of many developing countries in Africa.

Another form of income for developing countries, somewhat related to foreign aid, is known as remittance. Remittance is the money immigrants send to help support their families in their home country. Though individual remittances may seem minor, remittances to developing countries totaled $429 billion in 2016, according to the World Bank. The World Bank's estimate of remittance for 2017 was $450 billion.

While the United States is a wealthier country and does not depend on aid from other countries, some countries have offered direct aid after natural disasters in the United States. In addition to being helpful, these offers show political goodwill. After Hurricane Harvey hit Texas in 2017, several countries that are not as wealthy as the United States offered help; for instance, Mexico offered boats and food, while Venezuela offered $5 million in aid. The United States does not accept all aid offers, but whoever is president at the time generally thanks the government that made the offer.

CRITICIZING THE WHITE SAVIOR COMPLEX

"The attitude that Africa needs to be saved from itself, by Westerners, can be traced back to colonialism and slavery ... It's such a simplified way to view an entire continent."—anonymous creators of the Barbie Savior Instagram account

Quoted in Zeba Blay, "White Savior Barbie' Hilariously Parodies Volunteer Selfies in Africa," *Huffington Post*, April 18, 2016. www.huffingtonpost.com/entry/white-savior-barbie-hilariously-parodies-volunteer-selfies-in-africa_us_570fd4b5e4b03d8b7b9fc464.

Not All Aid Is Effective

Aid to developing countries is criticized for many reasons. Critics claim that development aid is sometimes counterproductive because it cannot sustain itself. They argue that rather than lessening poverty, development aid promotes poverty by encouraging dependency. Also, development aid from wealthy countries sometimes targets projects that may be inappropriate at the local level. A hydroelectric power project on the Tigris

River in Turkey was highly controversial for that reason. The project, begun in 2006, was funded by development aid from an international group led by a Swiss company. The project was supposed to provide electricity and jobs for thousands of people; however, construction of the reservoir flooded many small settlements along the Tigris and displaced 80,000 Turkish Kurds from their homes.

In his book *Toxic Charity*, urban activist Robert Lupton explained that although direct aid can be helpful, it can also be harmful when it is not combined with education and resources to make people in developing countries self-sufficient. In an interview with *Huffington Post*, he explained why help from churches and charities can sometimes have the opposite effect:

> *Typically, the giving is one-way: those of us with the resources give to those with a lack of resources. One-way giving tends to make the poor objects of pity, which harms their dignity. It also erodes their work ethic and produces a dependency that is unhealthy both for the giver and the recipient …*
>
> *The feel-good experience draws us back in. In our newsletters about mission trips we report how wonderful and grateful the people are, but what we don't hear are the ways that the trips damage people behind the scenes.*[31]

According to Lupton, one-way giving is generally only helpful in emergency situations such as the aftermath of natural disasters. To help people lift themselves out of poverty, the most effective projects are those that involve the people being helped in the process and teach them skills that allow them to help themselves in the long term.

NGOs are divided into categories. Not all NGOs support small projects. Oxfam, for example, is an NGO that helps people develop sustainable agricultural techniques or methods of obtaining clean water. Other NGOs raise awareness about specific causes, such as women's rights or the environment.

Direct Food Aid Is Complicated

Direct food aid generates similar controversy. Critics argue that food donations deepen the hunger crisis rather than improve it.

Farmers in the United States and other wealthy nations are paid subsidies, or fees, to produce surplus grain and other crops. This extra food is then shipped to poor countries, where it is donated or sold cheaply to local citizens. Income from these food sales helps fund organizations that battle poverty. However, since these surplus foods are so cheap, critics claim that their sale undermines local farmers. They cannot compete with the inexpensive donated food from abroad. Many critics of this so-called "food dumping" argue that it benefits American farmers but harms the security of local farmers; however, others dispute this charge.

In 2007, CARE, one of the world's largest humanitarian organizations, turned down $45 million in federal aid to fund its programs because the money was raised by selling subsidized American crops in African countries. CARE claimed that the sale of these products unfairly competed with the crops of African farmers, making it difficult for them to sell their produce; however, the Christian charity World Vision and 14 other groups criticized CARE's refusal to accept federal aid. They say that food aid keeps money in developing countries, stabilizes prices, and helps fund charitable organizations. They argue that providing inexpensive products to feed the poor is the primary goal of selling subsidized farm products. If shipping and agriculture businesses also profit, those profits are a secondary benefit, not reason to criticize or halt the practice altogether.

Loans: Benefit or Burden?

Much of the aid given by wealthy nations takes the form of loans. Countries that accept loans agree to certain conditions. These conditions might include deadlines for repayment, interest rates, and other terms. Debt repayment places a heavy burden on developing countries. Resources that might pay for health care and education are diverted to loan repayment. Sometimes conditions appear to benefit both the donor country and the recipient, but in reality, these loans increase hardship for struggling people of poor countries. For example, a donor country might anticipate a future grain shortage and require that the recipient promise to sell back its grain at reduced prices. Farmers in the recipient country have no choice but to sell their crops at set prices to their own governments to satisfy that condition.

Does Poverty Cause Terrorism?

It is not uncommon to hear or read that terrorists act out of frustration at being excluded from the benefits of wealth; however, evidence suggests that terrorists and their home countries are often not poor. In fact, of the 50 poorest countries in the world, only Afghanistan, Bangladesh, and Yemen are commonly associated with terrorism. On the individual level, the 19 hijackers who flew planes into the World Trade Center in New York City on September 11, 2001, were middle class, well-educated citizens of Saudi Arabia. Osama bin Laden, the much-feared leader and founder of al-Qaeda, the international Islamic terrorist group, was from one of the wealthiest families in the Middle East. Furthermore, a study of suicide bombers from 1987 to 2002 found that most are relatively well-off and educated. An essay by former Harvard researcher Efraim Benmelech and his colleague Claude Berrebi of the RAND Corporation pointed out that the deadliest terrorist activities, such as suicide bombings, are often assigned to the most highly educated and dedicated volunteers. Cait Murphy of *Fortune* magazine concluded, "There are many good reasons to worry about poverty, and to take action to alleviate it. But ending terrorism is not one of them."[1]

1. Cait Murphy, "The Poverty/Terror Myth," *Fortune*, March 13, 2007. archive.fortune.com/2007/03/13/magazines/fortune/pluggedin_murphy_terror.fortune/index.htm?section=money_email_alerts.

Some critics, who are suspicious of government aid, claim the real purpose of foreign aid is to manipulate a recipient country's politics. This was a common view in the 1950s when the United States and the Soviet Union represented the conflict between democracy and communism. Both countries were accused of using foreign aid as a tool to gain political allies. In recent decades, criticism has also been aimed at the International Monetary Fund and the World Bank. Critics believe the primary motive that fuels aid from these organizations is the creation of new markets for products exported by industrialized countries. While people in developing countries may also benefit, critics claim that the well-being of the poor is not the prime motive.

A COUNTRY NEEDS ALL OF ITS PEOPLE

"In many poor countries, the greatest unexploited re-
source isn't oil fields or veins of gold; it is the women
and girls who aren't educated and never become a
major presence in the formal economy."
—Nicholas Kristof, *New York Times* columnist,
and Sheryl WuDunn, journalist, author,
and businesswoman

Nicholas Kristof and Sheryl WuDunn, "The Women's Crusade," *New York Times Magazine*, August 23,
2009, www.nytimes.com/2009/08/23/magazine/23Women-t.html

Cause and Effect

Controversy about whether aid hurts or helps developing countries is ongoing; however, there is no doubt that many countries, such as Rwanda, Tanzania, and Mozambique in Africa, are
largely aid dependent. As economies falter, wealthy countries in
the West scale back on donations that support these economies.
In a familiar chain of causes and consequences, less aid results in
political instability. Political instability results in loss of income
from tourism, an important source of income in some countries.
Farmers threatened by ethnic conflict may be afraid to farm.
This is particularly true in some African countries that depend
on sales of high-end coffee, teas, and tropical flowers.

President Lyndon B. Johnson believed it was possible to defeat
poverty; however, the population of the world has more than
doubled since his administration, and poverty shows little sign
of abating. To those who struggle against the suffering caused by
poverty, the point is not whether the sustainable development
goals will be met by target year 2030, but whether they can
be met at all. World crises present unexpected obstacles, and
some situations have deteriorated rather than improved. Still,
it is clear that people from world leaders to ordinary citizens
cannot turn away from the suffering of humanity. Thousands of
organizations, private individuals, businesses, and government
leaders devote billions of dollars and untold amounts of energy
working to improve health care and bring safe water and food to
those who need them. That in itself is cause for hope.

CHAPTER 4

Climate and Poverty

As pointed out in the Sustainable Development Goals, the relationship between poverty and the environment is an important one to consider. Depending on where someone lives, they face different challenges. In some places, hot and humid weather increase the prevalence of diseases such as malaria. In others, it is staying warm that is the challenge. As climate change affects weather patterns, the dangers of floods, hurricanes, blizzards, and storms will affect some communities more than others, depending on location.

In addition to these challenges, people everywhere rely on the earth for the resources to grow food, create power, and provide for their needs. In areas where the environment is struggling, the people struggle as well. If the water is polluted, crop growth will be stunted. If the forests are cut down, people who relied on the trees for their livelihood will suffer. For those living in poverty, even small changes to the environment can be devastating.

For these reasons, taking care of the environment is a crucial element of fighting poverty. Those with the fewest resources experience the effects of environmental strain the quickest. Rising global temperatures have the greatest impact on impoverished communities living near the earth's equator. It is important to make sure efforts to fight poverty are as environmentally friendly as possible, otherwise these efforts could create more problems than they solve.

Urbanization

Many cities have a difficult time meeting the energy, water, and waste management needs of their growing populations. As small farming becomes less profitable, people leave rural areas and move to cities to seek both high- and low-wage jobs. These areas may become crowded, which creates environmental problems. According to Cities Alliance, a global coalition dedicated to reducing poverty in cities, "The poverty of the urban environment is not a marginal issue: there is a clear and consistent relationship between weak systems of governance, corruption, urban poverty, and a degraded urban environment."[32] In the best cases, careful planning and well-run government agencies can absorb growing populations. Nonetheless, in many developing nations, both are often absent.

Without urban planning, impoverished people set up living space wherever they can find it. They might gather on land that is unsafe or unstable, which no one else will take. According to Cities Alliance, the land that is settled in this way by the poor is often "sensitive land that should be left undisturbed, along rivers or canals, in protected areas, on marginal and dangerous land, and on watersheds needed for supplying water to critical reservoirs."[33] Once slums, or areas of substandard housing, are established in these sensitive areas, the cycle of urban poverty and environmental damage begins. Raw, or untreated, sewage is dumped into lakes, rivers, and coastal waters. Children play in these waterways, and families have little access to clean, safe water. Cities Alliance estimates that two-thirds of the raw sewage on the planet is left untreated, creating health hazards for humans and the environment alike.

Although the United States has better resources than developing countries, those resources do not always get properly distributed. Many cities have a large homeless problem, resulting in "tent cities" in places such as Anaheim, California, and Seattle, Washington. These are areas where homeless people set up tents and tarps; as in developing countries, they are generally seen in places that are not ideal, such as along riverbanks and under freeway overpasses. Rather than offering aid to these people, local residents often see them as a nuisance. An article published in *America* magazine noted that in Anaheim in 2017:

> More than 13,000 residents had signed a petition calling for the removal of the 400 or so people living along the riverbed, an effort that had been facilitated [started] by paid organizers.

Orange County had also not only refused to install portable toilets in the area but removed others that had been paid for and installed by local religious organizations. Proposed transitional shelters have been repeatedly stopped by residents that do not want them in their neighborhoods, and the city had already removed bus benches across from Disneyland because homeless people were sleeping on them.[34]

This reaction shows that while many people who live in the United States support helping the poor in other countries, they often have a blind spot when it comes to the poor in their own country. In fact, the inequality is so great and the response to it has been so inadequate that in December 2017, the UN sent a representative to investigate the problem—something almost unheard-of for a developed country. The representative, Philip Alston, gathered data in California, West Virginia, Georgia, Puerto Rico, and Washington, D.C., and prepared a report for the UN about possible human rights violations in those areas. According to the website Quartz, Alston focused

closely on specific poverty-related issues that have risen in the US in recent years, including an outbreak of hookworm in Alabama— a disease linked with poverty and poor sanitary conditions typically found in South Asia and Subsaharan Africa.

Other subjects of investigation include voter suppression, gaps in civil rights, sanitation (including water quality), and access to health care. All this with the understanding that poverty is a result of political choices: "Civilized governments don't say 'go and make it on your own, and if you can't, then bad luck,'" explains Alston. "The idea of human rights is that people have basic dignities that is the role of the government to ensure that no one falls below a decent level."[35]

On December 15, Alston delivered his report, which outlined several key findings:

- A tax reform bill proposed by Congress would increase the already large gap in income inequality between the richest and poorest Americans as well as decreasing the benefits many impoverished Americans depend on.

- Although the United States has a lot of wealth and technology available, it is not being used to help its poorest citizens.

- Alston saw many negative aspects that could easily be corrected—for instance, he met adults who no longer had teeth because the health insurance they could afford did not cover dental care, so they could not afford to see a dentist.

- Alston also saw positive aspects, such as local government officials who were committed to passing laws in their districts that would help impoverished people. He also saw people volunteering where the government failed to help—for example, he cited a community health project in Charleston, West Virginia, where doctors, dentists, and other medical professionals served patients for free.

- The United States has severe problems compared to other developed countries, especially regarding health. For example, Alston noted that although the United States spends more on health care than any other developed country, there are fewer hospital beds and doctors available than in other countries, forcing some people to go without necessary medical care.

- Although the United States has agreed with the UN that economic and social security are basic human rights, the government has consistently denied programs that would help its citizens achieve those rights. For example, although most developed countries have universal health care programs, the United States has consistently rejected plans to develop one.

- Many people in the United States equate economic status with morality—they believe people are either rich or poor because they deserve to be. The rich are viewed as hardworking and determined, while the poor are seen as lazy and wasteful. Because of these false perceptions, many politicians as well as members of the general public oppose welfare programs that would help the poor and support tax programs that allow the wealthiest citizens to pay less in taxes—based on the idea that they have worked hard for their money and deserve to keep it—placing the burden of taxation on people who already have the least money.

- Most of the poverty issues in the United States could be solved if politicians worked toward this goal.

- The United States is a democracy, which means people can vote on which policies they want to see implemented. However, certain voting policies in the country either openly or secretly prevent the poorest people from voting; for example, some places require someone to show a driver's license in order to vote, so people who have never learned to drive—a common state among poor people who do not have the money for driver's education classes or access to a car—also cannot vote. This means impoverished people are unable to express their support for policies that would help them. People who do not benefit from these policies are less likely to vote for them, especially if they are unaware of the extent of poverty in their own country.

More and more people move to the capital city of Mongolia, Ulaanbaatar, each year. There is not enough housing in the city to support them, so they must live in polluted and crowded districts on the outskirts of the city.

These are only a few of the many problems Alston outlined in his report. Others include the disorganized state of the criminal justice system, the more severe burden on women than on men, the unproven belief that the poor and disabled do not need government assistance and primarily try to "scam the system," and punishment instead of treatment for people who are addicted to drugs.

CUTTING BACK ON CARS

"As long as we try to combat poverty within a system that is encouraging people to use food to power their cars rather than to drive less, to use more mass transit, or to demand vehicles that get better gas mileage, we are never going to be successful."
—Thomas L. Friedman, author and journalist

Thomas L. Friedman, *Hot, Flat, and Crowded*. New York, NY: Farrar, Straus, & Giroux, 2008, p. 183

The Importance of Cities in the Fight Against Poverty

The steady rise in urban population does not necessarily spell doom for the planet, though urban growth presents major environmental challenges. In the first decades of the 21st century, cities occupy about 3 percent of the surface of the earth, but they house more than half of the world's population. It is estimated that by 2050, 70 percent of the world will live in urban environments. The more people are living in an area, the more resources they consume and the more pollution they create. While these facts make it seem like cities are the cause of environmental destruction, some experts believe that cities may actually hold the key to saving the environment. Achim Steiner, the administrator of the United Nations Development Programme, said, "It is imperative, therefore, to view cities—and the mayors who run them—as essential allies in the struggle against urban environmental decay and poverty, not as their cause."[36] He pointed out that urban dwellers generally have higher incomes than those who

Cities and towns are responsible for 80 percent of carbon dioxide emissions.

live in outlying areas. Also, businesses and city dwellers share markets and services, which helps cover costs. Well-run cities generate funds that can be used to help reduce poverty and improve quality of life. However, in order for this to happen, city dwellers must become allies in the quest to improve city life. This means taking steps to replace poor, dangerous areas with safe, low-cost housing, improve educational and employment opportunities, and make important services such as transportation accessible to everyone. This will require governments as well as citizens to make a dedicated effort toward creating change.

The Importance of Forests

Unfortunately, many places in the world lack the organization to plan carefully for growth. The disorganization adds to poverty and damages the environment. Haiti, an island country in the Caribbean and one of the poorest countries in the Western Hemisphere, stands out as a country that has devastated its environment in its effort to provide for its population. More than 80 percent of Haitians live below the poverty line, and many of them cannot afford even basic necessities.

Some people link Haiti's misfortunes directly to the loss of its forests, which have been logged extensively to provide wood for cooking. The loss of its forests leaves the exposed land vulnerable to hurricanes and landslides. In 2008, for example, four hurricanes blew through Haiti, leaving thousands dead; many died in landslides that resulted from the combination of vast rains and the loss of tree cover. The same hurricanes resulted in fewer

Natural disasters have an even greater impact on those who are already struggling to survive.

than 100 deaths in nearby Florida. In a familiar cycle, the consequences of being poor create conditions that perpetuate poverty.

Using wood as fuel creates other environmental problems for the poor. The indoor air pollution that results from cooking over wood fires is unhealthy. The World Health Organization (WHO) estimates that more than 4 million people die each year from respiratory illnesses that result from indoor cooking fumes.

Deforestation throughout the world causes a wide range of problems for people and the planet. Scientists express concern for the loss of biodiversity as rain forest plants and animals lose their habitat. Deforestation in South America and Africa also threatens the world with climate change because tropical trees are able to absorb carbon emissions that cause climate change.

A 2009 *New York Times* article by Elisabeth Rosenthal titled "In Brazil, Paying Farmers to Let the Trees Stand" described the massive deforestation that has taken place as Brazilian rain forests are cleared to make room for profitable crops of soybeans and corn as well as grazing land for cattle. The Brazilian farmers receive only part of the profit. Much of the wealth flows to the multinational companies that export the crops across the globe. American companies such as Cargill and Archer Daniels Midland purchase much of Brazil's soybean crop to feed cows in Europe and China.

Landowners in Brazil must weigh the loss of biodiversity and climate change against immediate benefits to themselves and their families. Though they value the environment, it is difficult for them to turn down substantial offers of cash from corporations to buy their land. Rosenthal

Cutting down towering trees in the Amazon rain forest (shown here) may provide a financial benefit in the short term, but in the long term, it could have a devastating impact on the environment.

illustrated the personal dilemma that faces Brazilians in Mato Grosso, the state of Brazil that is considered the global epicenter of deforestation. She described Pedro Alves Guimarães, a 73-year-old farmer who migrated to the rain forests there in 1964 in search of free land. He built a hut in the forest and raised cattle. Rosenthal explained, "While he regrets the loss of the forest, he has welcomed amenities like the school built a few years ago that his grandchildren attend, or the electricity put in last year that allowed him to buy his first freezer."[37] These are hard choices. They pit immediate benefits to people and their families against environmental damage that may not be revealed for many years.

COMPLICATED CONNECTIONS

"When we try to pick out anything by itself, we find it hitched to everything else in the universe."
—John Muir, founder of the Sierra Club

Quoted in Harold Wood, "John Muir Misquoted," Sierra Club, accessed December 20, 2017. vault.sierraclub.org/john_muir_exhibit/writings/misquotes.aspx

Affected by Natural Disasters

There are reasons why natural disasters affect the poor disproportionately. They frequently occupy low-lying land that is prone to floods. Their shelters are generally less secure, which makes them more prone to destruction in earthquakes and landslides. Most people in developing countries do not own insurance to help them rebuild if their homes are destroyed.

Hurricane Katrina provides a prime example. In August 2005, Hurricane Katrina struck the Gulf Coast of the United States. The hurricane devastated parts of Louisiana, Mississippi, and Florida. At least 1,800 people died. Evacuation of the city of New Orleans, Louisiana, stalled because many people did not have transportation or money to purchase transportation out of the city. State and federal efforts to provide transportation and evacuate the city were poorly organized and inefficient.

When Capitalism Is Harmful

For middle-class people, the first step to saving money and helping the environment is generally to use less. For instance, if someone wants to save up for a vacation, they might choose to temporarily give something else up, such as their daily coffee from a coffee shop; in addition to helping them save money, they are not throwing away a disposable cup every day, so they are generating less waste. However, the poor already consume less energy, use less water, occupy less land, and generate less waste. Low-income populations build houses from recycled or discarded materials. They walk or ride bicycles rather than drive cars, and they buy fewer goods, resulting in less factory waste. In fact, the UN estimates that the wealthiest 20 percent of the world's people account for almost 90 percent of the world's consumption of resources.

In at least one case, this careful use of resources has actually harmed impoverished people rather than helping them. Suez, a French company, won a contract in La Paz, Bolivia, when it promised to expand the water network to poor neighborhoods outside the city. One such area is El Alto, home to three-quarters of a million people, mostly poor Indians who have relocated from the Andes Mountains. In an article called "Letter from Bolivia: Leasing the Rain," journalist William Finnegan described why the project failed: "It seemed that the people in El Alto weren't using enough water. Accustomed to Andean peasant life, they were extremely careful with water, never wasting a drop, and they continued to be so even after they had taps installed in their homes. This was good for conservation, but it was bad for Suez's bottom line [profits]."[1] The company raised its rates, and the general satisfaction with the water project deteriorated. Complaints escalated into a massive demonstration, and in 2005, the government canceled the contract with Suez. An official from the World Bank blamed the failure on thrifty water use by the people of El Alto. This incident shows how capitalism—an economic policy concerned with making the most profit possible—can sometimes be a barrier to economic development in poorer countries.

1. William Finnegan, "Letter from Bolivia: Leasing the Rain," *New Yorker*, April 8, 2002. www.newyorker.com/archive/2002/04/08/020408fa_FACT1.

The residents of New Orleans most affected by Hurricane Katrina lived mostly in the lower Ninth Ward, a section of the city that is home to a largely poor African American population. At the time, many blamed the Federal Emergency Management Agency (FEMA), which gives aid to American citizens after disasters, for its slow response to the emergency. They claimed that underlying racism and classism were at the core of the issue, since the people who needed help were mostly poor and black. Television networks broadcast images around the world of thousands of people waiting for days in the New Orleans Superdome without food, water, or adequate sanitation.

Similarly, when Puerto Rico was hit by Hurricane Maria in September 2017, what little aid it received from the federal government was slow in coming. Many people noticed the difference between the response to Puerto Rico and the response to mainland states, and only about half of Americans know that although Puerto Rico is not a state, its people are American citizens, entitled to the same aid the government gave the major cities of Houston, Texas, and Miami, Florida, when they were hit by hurricanes only weeks before Puerto Rico was. CNN compared the response to these three hurricanes, including the action of FEMA:

> **Hurricane Harvey:** *For Hurricane Harvey, FEMA had supplies and personnel positioned in Texas before the storm made landfall on August 25. Within days, the number of FEMA employees, other federal agencies, and the National Guard deployed topped 31,000, FEMA said. In addition, FEMA supplied 3 million meals and 3 million liters of water to Texas to be distributed to survivors.*

> **Hurricane Irma:** *Even more federal personnel responded to Hurricane Irma when it made landfall in Florida on September 10. More than 40,000 federal personnel, including 2,650 FEMA staff, were in place by September 14. In addition, FEMA had transferred 6.6 million meals and 4.7 million liters of water to states in the Southeast after Irma as of the 14th.*

> **Hurricane Maria:** *By comparison, Puerto Rico and the Virgin Islands have seen much fewer personnel since Hurricane Maria hit, according to FEMA. In a tweet on Monday [September 25, 2017],*

FEMA said that more than 10,000 federal staff were on the ground in Puerto Rico and the Virgin Islands assisting search and rescue and recovery efforts.[38]

As of January 2018, Puerto Rico was still mostly without electricity and officials estimated full power would not be restored until at least February—the longest blackout in U.S. history. Food, water, and adequate medical care were also hard to come by, endangering many lives. The storm also left many without jobs, meaning that even if there were a lot of resources available, people would not be able to afford them. Leaving the island is next to impossible even for those who can afford a plane ticket; according to *Vox,* "Some airlines reportedly have waiting lists of 20,000 people."[39]

Some believe the reason the response to Puerto Rico's problems has been so slow is that many of its people were living in poverty even before the hurricane hit. President Donald Trump made several references to Puerto Rico being in debt

Being without electricity for a few hours is often not a problem, but over a long period of time, it can have serious negative effects.

LACK OF RESPONSE

"One marker for underdevelopment is the lack of a first response system. When you saw the television reports on the tsunami [in Thailand], you never saw ambulances arriving to help afterward. The main image of [the terrorist attacks on] 9/11 in New York was that of first responders rushing in to save lives."
—John Mutter, Department of Earth and Environmental Sciences at Columbia University

Quoted in Claudia Dreifus, "Earth Science Meets Social Science," *New York Times*, March 14, 2006. www.nytimes.com/2006/03/14/science/14conv.html?_r=1&scp=1&sq=%22earth+science+meets+social+science%22&st=nyt source?

when he discussed sending aid—a topic that did not come up in his response to the other two hurricanes. This debt is partially due to trade agreements with the mainland United States that charge Puerto Ricans high taxes on goods shipped to the island. Rebuilding Puerto Rico will be expensive, which may make the government reluctant to get too involved.

Oil spills do not just hurt animals such as this bird; they also can impact the lives of impoverished people living in nearby communities.

The Impact of Spills

Not all environmental disasters result from natural forces. Human error is also a cause. Often, the poor suffer disproportionately from these disasters, too. Their poverty makes them more vulnerable because their livelihoods are less secure. When accidents happen, the poor have fewer financial resources to withstand and recover from hardship, and sometimes the effects are not apparent until several years later.

That is what happened in Prince William Sound, Alaska, in March 1989, when the supertanker *Exxon Valdez* ran aground and spilled 11 million gallons (41,639,529.6 L) of oil into the sea, killing thousands of seabirds as well as sea otters, harbor seals, killer whales, and billions of salmon and herring eggs. Exxon blamed the ship's captain and spent more than $3.5 billion in the immediate aftermath cleaning up the 1,300 miles (2,080 km) of oily shoreline, rehabilitating wildlife, and compensating people who claimed damages. However, a few years later, both the salmon and herring industries collapsed, plunging into poverty thousands of fishermen and others whose livelihoods depend on the fishing industry. Exxon denied that the spill resulted in the death of the fish, but many scientists disagree.

The needs of those who live in poverty are urgent. Hunger and disease are immediate. The consequences of ignoring them are terrible. The dangers to the environment are urgent, too. Climate change, pollution, and loss of biodiversity occur more slowly, but the dangers they pose are serious. The challenge facing scientists, governments, the UN, environmental organizations, and others is to find a way to tackle both the immediate hazards of poverty and the long- and short-term perils to the environment. The goal is to lessen the damage to each without harming the other in the process.

CHAPTER 5

Poverty in the 21st Century

The fight against poverty has been going on for a long time, but today the battle is greatly aided by new and innovative technology. The internet allows people to connect around the world unlike anything else in history, and cell phones increase the communication power of many individuals. Society has powerful medicines and vaccines that can virtually eradicate many diseases as well as new means of generating electricity from the sun and the wind. Genetic engineering has created crops that can resist pests and droughts, trade has become faster due to shipping innovations, and advances in engineering have improved the infrastructure in many places. However, there are many places in the world where these improvements have yet to take hold. Nevertheless, these innovations may prove to be just what is needed to defeat poverty once and for all.

Solutions: Bottom Up or Top Down?

One approach to combating poverty is to search for practical and inexpensive ways to solve the challenges of everyday life. People living in impoverished regions often face challenges meeting basic needs—water must be carried for long distances, food must be preserved, and fuel must be gathered and stored for cooking.

Each year, the International Development Innovation Network (IDIN) brings people together from around the globe in a month-long International Development Design Summit. The purpose of the summit is to design technological solutions to problems that plague the developing world. Paul Polak, author of *Out of Poverty: What Works When Traditional Approaches Fail?*, emphasized that solutions must begin not in government offices, universities, or laboratories, but by assessing the real needs of the people facing the problems. Polak emphasized that to improve lives, technology needs to be simple and mesh with the lifestyles of the people for whom it is designed. He compared the best designs to a drip irrigation system. As a gardener or a farmer cultivates more land, pieces are added to enlarge the system. Thus a good design provides the basis for future innovation and expansion. According to Polak, most technology is not designed to help or serve the poor. Currently, 90 percent of research and development goes to technologies that serve the wealthiest 10 percent of the population.

In the United States, some people support a theory favored by President Ronald Reagan called "trickle-down economics"— sometimes nicknamed "Reaganomics" because of how strongly Reagan supported it. *USA Today* explained how trickle-down economics is supposed to work: "Lowering taxes for businesses and wealthy individuals leaves more cash in their pockets, spurring more investment and hiring, and the faster growth generates enough new tax income to pay for the cuts."[40] Supporters say this theory can help the American economy and create more jobs, while opponents have strongly criticized it. Even the opinion of economic experts is divided.

While Donald Trump was running for president in 2016, he stated that he was going to use the trickle-down theory to create jobs. According to "Ike Brannon, senior visiting fellow at the Cato Institute and economic advisor for [Senator] John McCain ... during his 2008 presidential run, 'If you make it cheaper to invest, ultimately, companies are going to grow and hire more people.'"[41] Jared Bernstein, former chief economist for Vice President Joe Biden and a senior fellow at the Center on Budget and Policy Priorities, disagreed, saying that it is unclear whether the tax cuts are what boosted the economy. He pointed out that

> President Bill Clinton "*significantly raised taxes and had bigger job gains than Reagan*" ... About 22 million jobs were created in the eight years Clinton was in office, and the economy grew an average 3.8% a year, helped, in part, by a tech boom that turbocharged business productivity. Despite tax cuts for the wealthy, the economy slipped into a deep recession in George W. Bush's term.[42]

Many experts say trickle-down economics can work, but only in specific circumstances—for instance, when taxes for the wealthy are very high, as they were in the 1980s. Additionally, trickle-down economics relies on business owners to invest their increased wealth into their companies, creating more jobs. In reality, wages have stagnated in recent years while the heads of companies—chief executive officers (CEOs)—have increased their own salaries. In 2015, *Huffington Post* reported on a study done by career review website Glassdoor, which reviewed information about CEOs' and workers' salaries from 2014. The study found that "the average pay ratio of CEO to median worker was 204-to-1 ... At the top of the list, four CEOs earn more than 1,000 times the salary of their median worker."[43] Many people criticize this gap, saying that CEOs could easily reduce poverty among their workers by cutting their own salaries and redistributing the savings. For example, the CEO of Mexican restaurant chain Chipotle, Steve Ells, "earned $28.9 million, or 1,522 times the median salary of $19,000"[44] that his workers received. In many places in the United States, $19,000 is not enough to live on. Critics say that if people such as Ells cut their salary by $2 million, they would still have more than enough to live on and so would their workers; some have called for an increased federal minimum wage. However, others say increasing the minimum wage is unnecessary. They claim that giving a restaurant worker $15 per hour would make them overpaid for the work they are doing and that raising the minimum wage would hurt the economy by placing an extra burden on companies, costing them more money and cutting into their profits, which would force them to raise prices, thereby negating any effect a higher salary may have had.

Other factors in the way the American economy functions contribute to poverty. Some companies lay off higher-paid workers so they can hire people who are willing to work for less; when someone is already living at or near the poverty line, they will generally take just about any salary they are offered, in contrast to someone who is wealthier and can afford to bargain for a higher wage. People who have been at a company for a long time are also less likely to get frequent raises the way they would in the past. This can contribute to poverty because the cost of living keeps rising, but in certain jobs, people's wages are not keeping pace with it. This means a salary that easily supported someone when they started working may no longer support them five years later. Some companies also cut costs by cutting employee benefits such as employee-sponsored health insurance, which negates any increased salary. Health insurance in the United States is very expensive, and when workers have to pay for it without any assistance from their employer, many find they are unable to afford more than basic coverage. The most basic plan may not cover certain things, such as surgery or hospital visits, which means that if an unexpected accident occurs, the employee may not be able to afford medical care even though they have insurance.

Opponents of the trickle-down theory of economics say the better policy is to put government money toward programs that help the poorest section of society, such as food stamps and other welfare programs. Critics of this view say welfare programs simply encourage people not to work, although studies have shown this to be false. Additionally, most government benefits are paid only to people who have or are actively looking for jobs; someone who is receiving welfare generally must show proof that they are applying to jobs and going to interviews, and welfare officials may follow up with companies to make sure the person is telling the truth. The debate about how best to combat poverty in the United States has been ongoing for decades and is not likely to be settled anytime soon.

THE BENEFIT OF SMARTPHONES

"Carrying a full-featured cellphone lessens your needs for other things, including a watch, an alarm clock, a camera, video camera, home stereo, television, computer, or for that matter, a newspaper. With the advent of mobile banking, cellphones have begun to replace wallets as well."
—Sara Corbett, journalist

Sara Corbett, "Can the Cellphone Help End Global Poverty?," New York Times Magazine, April 13, 2008. www.nytimes.com/2008/04/13/magazine/13anthropology-t.html

Access to Information

Engineering technology is certainly not new. Technology provided ancient civilizations with the tools needed to build the pyramids and create high-tech irrigation systems. However, in a world increasingly dependent on access to information, solutions to poverty may not rest in engineering designs at all—even new and unusual ones. Instead, many experts believe solutions to poverty will be found in improved access to information via the internet. In fact, Polak credited young people with suggesting some of the most effective solutions. He pointed out that they are less constrained by traditional ideas. The same technology that most American teenagers rely on to network with their friends and play games may hold the key to overcoming persistent poverty.

Access to the internet can have many benefits for impoverished people.

In late 2008 and early 2009, Barack Obama, then the newly elected president of the United States, worked to persuade Congress to pass a $900 billion program to stimulate the economy as a measure against the escalating worldwide financial crisis. The money was intended to help struggling homeowners and businesses, rescue banks and other financial institutions from bankruptcy, and thereby boost the economy. One percent of the stimulus package—or $9 billion—was set aside to expand broadband internet service to rural and underserved areas of the country, which are areas that tend to be the poorest.

Opinions varied widely about the value of this spending. *New York Times* reporter David Herszenhorn, in his outline of the controversy, described the advocates' viewpoint: "Proponents say it will create jobs, build crucial infrastructure and expand the information highway to every corner of the land."[45] Furthermore, they claimed it would streamline government bureaucracy and make it easier and more efficient to administer public assistance. Increased internet access would also expand market opportunities for small businesses and provide increased access to online health care and distance learning. The internet expands the ability of adults to find jobs and improve their literacy. Children in underserved schools benefit from connection to libraries, news sources, and the wealth of information available to students who are already connected.

Others were skeptical, saying the project was too expensive. In 2011, *Forbes* contributor Nick Schulz examined the effects of the internet stimulus:

> No one is against expanded access to broadband. And in rural areas especially, where there might be less market incentive to provide access, maybe there's a role for government to play. The question for prudent policymakers is how much such a project should cost and who should bear the cost. Surely there is some price that's too high to justify expanding access ...

> [Researchers] Eisenach and Caves looked at three areas that received stimulus funds, in the form of loans and direct grants, to expand broadband access in Southwestern Montana, Northwestern Kansas, and Northeastern Minnesota ...

> So how much did it cost per unserved household to get them broadband access? A whopping $349,234, or many multiples of household income, and significantly more than the cost of a home itself.[46]

Schulz also noted that in the Montana area, only seven houses had no internet access at all, making the cost there about $7 million of government funds spent per household. Many people agree that although internet access is important, this money might have been better spent on other projects.

Arguments focus on how to expand internet access and who should benefit from federal tax dollars. Many critics mistrust the motives of powerful wireless communications companies such as Verizon, which stand to receive hundreds of millions of dollars in tax credits. Others believe requirements that specify that everyone have access to new networks discourage smaller companies from applying for the funds. These companies are cautious about spending limited resources to develop networks that other companies will access at no cost. The details are still unclear, but whatever the outcome, it will take many years to develop the necessary infrastructure to provide the internet to outlying areas.

Expanding the Reach of the Internet

As proponents and critics debated the fine points of the U.S. plan, a 10,500-mile (17,000 km) fiber optic cable opened in 2009 that provided internet access to millions of people in southern and eastern Africa. SEACOM, a group composed mostly of African investors, financed the submarine cable. It was the first of 10 cable connections planned to link Africa with Europe, Asia, and the Middle East. The SEACOM cable provides internet service that is 10 times faster than the old single cable, which had not been updated since 2002. News of the cable was welcomed by many who struggle against poverty, particularly after a 2009 World Bank report directly linked economic growth to improved access to information and communication technology. The new technology enabled businesses in Africa to establish call centers similar to those in India and communicate with businesses and clients overseas. As of 2017, SEACOM is continuing to expand its access.

It could be many years before less expensive broadband connections are available to individuals, however. Étienne Lafougère, general manager for the company that is building the majority of the submarine cables in Africa, explained the delay. He said access depends on local internet service providers adding cables to the main system to reach isolated areas. Referring to the internet, Lafougère said, "We are building the highways; then you have to build roads and secondary roads, and that usually takes more time."[47]

Andrew Mwenda, a Ugandan journalist and social worker, believes technology offers an alternative to traditional aid. He has been an outspoken critic of traditional aid to Africa and believes that foreign aid only furthers Africa's dependence and passivity. He echoed the feelings of many when he said, "What man has ever become rich by holding out a begging bowl?"[48] Mwenda pointed to the $500 billion in international aid to Africa in the past 50 years to underscore his criticism. He claimed that foreign aid benefits governments and charities instead of the sick and poor. Mwenda urged Africans to start small businesses, and he called upon Americans to provide low-interest loans and mortgages directly to African entrepreneurs.

However, one West African businessman believes that a combination of aid and technology is more realistic. Alieu Conteh, the former chairman of Vodacom Congo, spoke about his experience starting the first digital network in Democratic Republic of the Congo. In 1999, Conteh introduced the Congolese Wireless Network, with 4,000 subscribers. In 2006, he sold the company to Vodacom. Now, more than 66 million users subscribe to Vodacom's service. Still, he said it is difficult to run a profitable business in Democratic Republic of the Congo. He claimed that the task was more difficult and more expensive than he thought it would be. It took more than 10 years to provide telecommunications to less than 10 percent of the country.

A FALSE CHOICE

"I think this choice between aid and entrepreneurship is false. If we wait for trade, it will take generations, and people need help now. On the other hand, only entrepreneurship can make us rich."
—Herman Chinery-Hesse, founder of Softtribe, a software development company in Ghana

Quoted in Jason Pontin, "What Does Africa Need Most: Technology or Aid?," *New York Times*, June 17, 2007. www.nytimes.com/2007/06/17/business/yourmoney/17stream.html?scp=1&sq=What%20 Does%20Africa%20Need%20Most:%20Technology%20 or%20Aid&st=c.

"Economic Growth Comes with an On/Off Switch"

It may seem as if the internet operates in a virtual world apart from the earth, but its power is decidedly earthbound. That power can be generated by the wind, by the sun as solar power, by water as hydroelectric power, by fossil fuels such as coal and oil, or through a variety of other methods, but regardless of how power is generated, no one has yet figured out how to bypass it altogether. As journalist Thomas Friedman put it, "Today more than ever, economic growth comes with an on/off switch."[49] Computers and the internet connect people to the world's intellectual resources: books, newspapers and news agencies, and people and their ideas. Computers spread information quickly and efficiently, but they cannot run without electricity.

Since energy grids are expensive to develop and operate, experts search for alternative ways to power technology. In some rural areas, old car batteries and makeshift solar panels serve that function. The fastest way for developing nations or impoverished regions to use the internet might be to bypass traditional sources of energy and head straight for energy fueled by the sun, wind, or water. Alternative energy accomplishes two objectives: It bypasses the necessity of building expensive and high-maintenance grids, and it safeguards the environment. Both contribute to the overriding goal of reducing the effects of poverty.

This concept can also be applied to telephone communications. It was not that long ago that making a phone call needed a connection—not only a cord attached to a telephone but a connection to a complex network of poles and lines. In some places, unused telephone poles and wires signal long-abandoned efforts to bring phone service to rural areas. Cell phones bypass that step. They connect without any lines at all. Moreover, that connection is what many people in remote regions desperately need. Many people in the United States see cell phones—especially smartphones—as a luxury, but in reality, they are a necessity in the 21st century. When a person or business does not have a phone, they miss out on job opportunities, connections with friends and family, and business growth, among other things.

Businesses that stand to profit from cell phones study the ways cell phones benefit the everyday lives of their users. In a feature story in *New York Times Magazine* in 2008, reporter Sara Corbett wrote about a conversation with a human behavior researcher for Nokia, the world's largest manufacturer of cell phones at the time. The researcher explained the importance to income and health that the ability to communicate has for people who are poor. Corbett summarized, "Having a call back number is having a fixed identity point, which, inside of populations that are constantly on the move—displaced by war, floods, drought, or faltering economies—can be immensely valuable both as a means of keeping in touch with home communities and as a business tool."[50]

Even the very poor invest a high percentage of their earnings on telecommunications. As a family's income grows—from $1 to $4 per day, for example—its spending on communication devices increases faster than spending in any other category, including health, education, and housing. People in developing countries spend limited resources on cell phones for different reasons than people in richer countries. Most people in the United States own cell phones, but they also own computers, televisions, and cars. They have many ways to communicate with others and receive news—for instance, by watching the evening news on TV. In developing countries, a cell phone may be the sole method available. A mother with a sick child can phone a clinic to find a doctor rather than walking three hours only to discover that the clinic is closed. Families can check on the whereabouts of other family members or use the cell phone to take care of errands more efficiently.

Cell phones can benefit people by helping them keep in touch with not only their families, but also business contacts.

Text messaging is also proving useful in developing countries. In some countries, health workers send text messages to remind patients to take medications. In others, people send text messages to ask professional advice anonymously about sensitive subjects such as AIDS, breast cancer, and sexually transmitted diseases (STDs). Health experts respond with confidential text messages.

Cell phones allow many people to become part of the formal economy. The phone functions as a mobile bank. People purchase cash credits through the post office, which are transferred onto their phones. They then use their phones to make payments or withdraw cash. This process was even used by aid organizations after the 2010 earthquake in Haiti. Millions of dollars were donated by cell phone users who texted keywords such as "HAITI" to transfer money from their cell phone accounts to organizations such as the American Red Cross.

It is not even necessary to own a cell phone to benefit from one, according to Polak, who is also the former president of iDE (previously known as International Development Enterprises), an organization that specializes in technology for small farmers in developing countries. In Nepal, iDE set up cooperatives to which local farmers bring their produce. The farmers often seek a cell phone owner to call around to find the best market for their produce. The farmers benefit, and the cell phone owner reaps part of the profit as payment for the service.

Corbett argued that cell phones can be used to promote independence from direct financial aid: "A cell phone in the hands of an Indian fisherman who uses it to grow his business—which presumably gives him more resources to feed, clothe, educate and safeguard his family—represents a way of empowering individuals by encouraging entrepreneurship."[51] Those who promote entrepreneurship prefer this bottom-up approach that is the direct outgrowth of the needs of the people who benefit. The reverse—a top-down approach—depends on filtering money from outside sources, such as foreign governments or charity organizations through a bureaucracy that distributes it. Some of the cell phone's most enthusiastic proponents are those who question the wisdom of the top-down approach—direct financial aid to poor countries.

Futuristic Solutions

Freeman Dyson, former physics professor at the Institute for Advanced Study in Princeton, New Jersey, also searches for ways to apply science and technology in a bottom-up manner. Dyson's devotion to social justice fuels his determination to find ways for science to reduce the effects of poverty. He claimed, "Rural poverty is one of the great evils of the modern world. The lack of jobs and economic opportunities in villages drives millions of people to migrate from villages into overcrowded cities. The continuing migration causes immense social and environmental problems in the major cities of poor countries."[52]

Dyson envisions the day that genetic engineering might stamp out rural poverty altogether. He suggests that once scientists master techniques of genetic engineering, they might manipulate genes to resolve many social problems. They might, for example, use genetic engineering to produce plants with black silicon leaves. These black-leaved plants would convert sunlight into energy with the same efficiency as solar cells—more than 10 times as efficiently as plants with green leaves. Not only would this create a new source of energy, it would help alleviate rural poverty. The cultivation of black-leaved crops and forests would be a growth industry ideally suited to rural settings, which would help reduce rural migration to cities, preventing overcrowding in those cities. Dyson foresees the ability to manipulate genetics as a source of endless possibilities, most of which are currently only imaginary. He envisions trees that produce liquid fuels, for example, and termites that digest rusty metal. He admits these developments seem outlandish but trusts science to solve society's most perplexing problems.

Dyson's ideas are often considered far-fetched. When his essay "Our Biotech Future" was published in the *New York Review of Books* in 2007, some letter writers disputed his ideas. Wendell Berry, a Kentucky writer, academic, and farmer, took issue with Dyson's notion that silicon-leaved plants might help reduce rural poverty. He pointed out that the countryside does not generally benefit when industrial technology sets up shop there. Instead, Berry claimed, "industries that are 'brought in' convey the local wealth *out*; otherwise they would not come."[53] Moreover, Berry explained that that the rural poor often have little control over the results of biotechnology. It is much more common for agribusinesses and biotech companies—not rural farmers—to benefit from new varieties of plants and genes that can be patented.

However, technology has already been used to create futuristic solutions. In 2017, the Borgen Project—a nonprofit organization dedicated to addressing the issues of poverty and hunger—wrote on its website about five high-tech anti-poverty solutions that won awards at an annual contest held by the Tech Museum of Innovation in San Jose, California:

- Equal Access International is an organization that "uses the power of media to tell human stories about those in poverty, raising awareness and shining a light on those who would otherwise be ignored."[54] In 2016, the organization partnered with UNICEF to produce a radio show that was broadcast in Nepal and "combines entertainment with education, teaching young people how to prevent becoming infected with HIV/AIDS."[55]

- International Development Enterprises—India (IDEI) created "an easy-to-use and cheap man-powered water pump resembling a tiered treadmill [so] farmers in India are able to extend their annual growing season with their own two feet."[56]

- Design Revolution (D-Rev) invented a lamp that is inexpensive to produce and lasts a long time. Called Brilliance, it cures jaundice—a yellow discoloration of the skin and eyes that is a sign of liver problems—in babies by "bathing them in a strong blue light … [It has] saved more than 175,000 infant lives across 41 countries."[57]

- Souktel, a start-up tech company, came up with a way to help people with flip phones, which are cheaper than smartphones but have fewer features—including limited or no internet access—connect and find jobs. The company "uses basic text messaging to link employers with candidates in regions where traditional communication is difficult, leading to job growth and greater economic gains ... Souktel turns text messages into miniature online job boards."[58]

- Angaza is a company that was created to give impoverished people who do not have electricity access to solar energy. While solar energy is cheaper and more sustainable in the long term, the solar panels and solar lamps themselves are generally too expensive for most people. "Instead of forcing people to pay up front for solar lamps, Angaza accepts micro-payments over time for energy while offering immediate access, similar to purchasing minutes on a cell phone. Once the purchase price of the device is reached, the lamp becomes the property of the user."[59] Not only does this give impoverished people access to sustainable electricity, it also helps the local economy.

These are only a few of the kinds of solutions that are being invented and implemented every day. Hopefully, as time goes on, this kind of unconventional thinking will provide answers to some of the problems associated with poverty.

Mutual Benefit

Ending poverty has obvious benefits for those who suffer within it, but ending poverty has benefits for those above the poverty line as well. If poverty were eliminated, all those people who now spend their energy trying to meet their basic survival needs would be able to focus their energy on loftier goals. How many people's talents are being used to find their next meal instead of using

Solar panels can bring technological advances to isolated communities.

those talents to cure cancer, invent new technology, or create great art? All of human society benefits when people reach out to help others living in poverty attain a better life.

While there is no single clear solution to the complex issue of poverty, there are many people working to find answers. The governments of various countries, the UN and World Bank, NGOs small and large, individual donors, and budding entrepreneurs all have a role to play in defeating the cycle of poverty. As new technology allows people to connect with and learn about the lives of those who live in many different places and who have many different experiences, the urgent need to fight poverty will become more apparent to everyone. Perhaps the daily struggles of poverty that plague so many around the world today will one day be a thing of the past.

NOTES

Chapter 1: Determining Poverty

1. Quoted in Louis Uchitelle, "How to Define Poverty? Let Us Count the Ways," *New York Times*, May 26, 2001. www.nytimes.com/2001/05/26/arts/how-to-define-poverty-let-us-count-the-ways.html.

2. Dr. David Gordon, "Indicators of Poverty & Hunger," University of Bristol, Poverty and Social Exclusion, December 12–14, 2005. www.poverty.ac.uk/sites/default/files/indicators-of-poverty-and-hunger_UNpoverty.pdf.

3. Gordon, "Indicators of Poverty & Hunger."

4. Anup Shah, "Poverty Around the World," Global Issues, updated November 12, 2011. www.globalissues.org/article/4/poverty-around-the-world.

5. Adam Smith, *An Inquiry into the Nature and Causes of the Wealth of Nations*. Hartford, CT: Lincoln & Gleason, 1804, p. 296.

6. Quoted in David Barsamian, "India Together: Interview with Amartya Sen," Alternative Radio, USA, September 2001. www.indiatogether.org/interviews/sen.htm.

7. "Address by Mr. Kofi Annan, Secretary General of the United Nations," United Nations Conference on Trade and Development, February 12, 2000. www.unctad.org/en/docs/ux_tdl365.en.pdf.

8. Larry Elliott and Charlotte Denny, "Top 1% Earn as Much as the Poorest 57%," *Guardian*, January 18, 2002. www.theguardian.com/business/2002/jan/18/research.socialsciences.

9. Howard W. French, "Lives of Grinding Poverty, Untouched by China's Boom," *New York Times*, January 13, 2008. query.nytimes.com/gst/fullpage.html?res=940DE7DD173A F930A25752C0A96E9C8B63.

Chapter 2: The Complex Cycle of Poverty

10. Jennifer Wills, "What Is the Economic Impact of Hosting the Olympics?," Investopedia, September 24, 2016. www.investopedia.com/articles/markets-economy/092416/ what-economic-impact-hosting-olympics.asp.

11. Wills, "What Is the Economic Impact of Hosting the Olympics?"

12. Robert I. Lerman, "Globalization and the Fight Against Poverty," Urban Institute, November 5, 2002. www.urban.org/ publications/410612.html.

13. "Remarkable Declines in Global Poverty, but Major Challenges Remain," World Bank, April 17, 2013. www.worldbank.org/en/news/press-release/2013/04/17/remarkable-declines-in-global-poverty-but-major-challenges-remain.

14. "The Tricky Work of Measuring Falling Global Poverty," *The Economist*, October 12, 2015. www.economist.com/ news/finance-economics/21673530-number-poor-people-declining-data-are-fuzzy-tricky-work-measuring-falling.

15. Lerman, "Globalization and the Fight Against Poverty."

16. "11 Facts About Sweatshops," DoSomething.org, accessed December 4, 2017. www.dosomething.org/us/facts/11-facts-about-sweatshops.

17. Lydia DePillis, "Trump Can't Decide if Outsourcing Is Good or Bad. Here's What Economists Say," *Washington Post*, March 3, 2016. www.washingtonpost.com/ news/wonk/wp/2016/03/03/trump-cant-decide-if-outsourcing-is-good-or-bad-heres-what-economists-say/?utm_term=.6008dd18189d.

18. Quoted in Thomas L. Friedman, *Hot, Flat, and Crowded*. New York, NY: Farrar, Straus & Giroux, p. 159.

19. Quoted in "Account for Oil Wealth," Human Rights Watch, July 9, 2009. www.hrw.org/en/news/2009/07/09/ equatorial-guinea-account-oil-wealth.

20. Quoted in Ramesh Jaura, "Corruption Nourishes Poverty," *InfoSud Human Rights Tribune*, September 24, 2008. www.infosud.org/Corruption-nourishes-poverty,3534.

21. Quoted in Jaura, "Corruption Nourishes Poverty."

22. Sonia Nazario, *Enrique's Journey*. New York, NY: Random House, 2007, p. 259.

23. Gillian B. White, "Poverty, Compounded," *The Atlantic*, April 16, 2016. www.theatlantic.com/business/archive/2016/04/ how-poverty-compounds/478539/.

Chapter 3: What Can Be Done About Poverty?

24. Quoted in "Did the United States Lose the War on Poverty?," Digital History, University of Houston. www.digitalhistory. uh.edu/historyonline/con_poverty.cfm.

25. "#Envision2030: 17 Goals to Transform the World for Persons with Disabilities," United Nations, accessed December 5, 2017. www.un.org/development/desa/disabilities/ envision2030.html.

26. "About 1Goal," 1Goal: Education for All, accessed December 20, 2017. www.join1goal.org/about-1GOAL.php.

27. "Gender Equality: A Cornerstone of Development," UNFPA. www.unfpa.org/gender/.

28. Quoted in Jon Boyle, "Better Water, Sanitation Keys to Easing Poverty: UN," Reuters, October 19, 2008. www.reuters. com/article/environmentNews/idUSTRE49I2IC20081019.

29. Ruth Ravve, "Flint Water Crisis: Some Residents Still Unable to Drink Tap Water Three Years Later," Fox News, November 3, 2017. www.foxnews.com/us/2017/11/03/flint-water-

crisis-michigan-residents-still-unable-to-drink-tap-water-three-years-later.html.

30. "Goal 17: Revitalize the Global Partnership for Sustainable Development," United Nations, accessed December 6, 2017. www.un.org/sustainabledevelopment/globalpartnerships/.

31. Quoted in Josef Kuhn, "Urban Activist and Author Relates Problems with Charity Work," *Huffington Post*, December 12, 2011. www.huffingtonpost.com/2011/10/12/robert-lupton-toxic-charity_n_1007751.html.

Chapter 4: Climate and Poverty

32. Cities Alliance, "Poverty of the Urban Environment," 2006, pp. 2–3. www.citiesalliance.org/sites/citiesalliance.org/files/Anual_Reports/poverty_urb_env_0.pdf.

33. Cities Alliance, "Poverty of the Urban Environment," p. 5.

34. Jim McDermott, "Tent City, USA: Southern California's Homelessness Crisis," *America*, October 16, 2017. www.americamagazine.org/politics-society/2017/09/18/tent-city-usa-southern-californias-homelessness-crisis.

35. Annalisa Merelli, "The UN Sent an Envoy to Investigate Extreme Poverty in the United States," Quartz, December 7, 2017. qz.com/1150167/the-united-nations-is-investigating-poverty-in-alabama-and-other-states/.

36. Cities Alliance, "Poverty of the Urban Environment."

37. Elisabeth Rosenthal, "In Brazil, Paying Farmers to Let the Trees Stand," *New York Times*, August 22, 2009. www.nytimes.com/2009/08/22/science/earth/22degrees.html.

38. Eric Levenson, "3 Storms, 3 Responses: Comparing Harvey, Irma and Maria," CNN, September 27, 2017. www.cnn.com/2017/09/26/us/response-harvey-irma-maria/index.html.

39. Brian Resnick and Eliza Barclay, "What Every American Needs to Know About Puerto Rico's Hurricane

Disaster," *Vox*, October 16, 2017. www.vox.com/science-and-health/2017/9/26/16365994/hurricane-maria-2017-puerto-rico-san-juan-humanitarian-disaster-electricty-fuel-flights-facts.

Chapter 5: Poverty in the 21st Century

40. Paul Davidson, "Can Trump Make 'Trickle-Down' Economics Work?," *USA Today*, November 13, 2016. www.usatoday.com/story/money/2016/11/11/can-trump-make-trickle-down-economics-work/93586144/.

41. Davidson, "Can Trump Make 'Trickle-Down' Economics Work?"

42. Davidson, "Can Trump Make 'Trickle-Down' Economics Work?"

43. Jenny Che, "Here's How Outrageous the Pay Gap Between CEOs and Workers Is," *Huffington Post*, August 27, 2015. www.huffingtonpost.com/entry/ceo-worker-pay-gap_us_55ddc3c7e4b0a40aa3acd1c9.

44. Che, "Here's How Outrageous the Pay Gap Between CEOs and Workers Is."

45. David M. Herszenhorn, "Internet Money in Fiscal Plan: Wise or Waste?," *New York Times*, February 3, 2009, p. A1.

46. Nick Schulz, "How Effective Was the 2009 Stimulus Program?," *Forbes*, July 5, 2011. www.forbes.com/sites/nickschulz/2011/07/05/how-effective-was-the-2009-stimulus-program/#3ab064d75cca.

47. Quoted in Cat Contiguglia, "New Undersea Cables to Expand Broadband in Africa," *New York Times*, August 9, 2009. www.nytimes.com/2009/08/10/technology/10cable.html.

48. Quoted in Jason Pontin, "What Does Africa Need Most: Technology or Aid?" *New York Times*, June 17, 2007. www.nytimes.com/2007/06/17/business/yourmoney/17stream.html.

49. Friedman, *Hot, Flat, and Crowded*, p. 158.

50. Sara Corbett, "Can the Cellphone Help End Global Poverty?," *New York Times Magazine*, April 13, 2008. www.nytimes.com/2008/04/13/magazine/13anthropology-t.html.

51. Corbett, "Can the Cellphone Help End Global Poverty?"

52. Freeman Dyson, "Our Biotech Future," *New York Review of Books*, July 19, 2007. www.nybooks.com/articles/2007/09/27/our-biotech-future-an-exchange/.

53. Wendell Berry, James P. Herman, Christopher B. Michael, and Freeman Dyson, "'Our Biotech Future': An Exchange," *New York Review of Books*, September 27, 2007. www.nybooks.com/articles/2007/07/19/our-biotech-future/

54. Dan Krajewski, "Top 5 Anti-Poverty Tech Solutions," The Borgen Project, April 20, 2017. borgenproject.org/top-5-anti-poverty-tech-solutions/.

55. Krajewski, "Top 5 Anti-Poverty Tech Solutions."

56. Krajewski, "Top 5 Anti-Poverty Tech Solutions."

57. Krajewski, "Top 5 Anti-Poverty Tech Solutions."

58. Krajewski, "Top 5 Anti-Poverty Tech Solutions."

59. Krajewski, "Top 5 Anti-Poverty Tech Solutions."

DISCUSSION QUESTIONS

Chapter 1: Defining Poverty

1. Why is it important to develop an agreement about how to define poverty?

2. What are some differences between developing and developed countries?

3. Why do you think some people use the terms "Global North" and "Global South" instead of "developed" or "developing"?

4. Explain why someone who lives in relative poverty may not seem poor to someone else.

Chapter 2: The Complex Cycle of Poverty

1. Explain Jared Diamond's concept of "geographic luck."

2. Why is outsourcing appealing to some companies, and what are some of the problems with it?

3. What are some of the factors that keep the cycle of poverty going? Can you think of more that were not discussed in the text?

Chapter 3: What Can Be Done About Poverty?

1. Describe the connections between the first three sustainable development goals and the rest of the sustainable development goals.

2. What is the 17th sustainable development goal, and why is it important?

3. What is the difference between development aid and direct aid?

4. Describe some ways in which developing countries are affected by economic crises.

Chapter 4: Climate and Poverty

1. Describe how cities impact the environment, both positively and negatively.

2. What are some benefits and costs of clearing the rain forest?

3. Why do the poor suffer disproportionately from natural disaster?

Chapter 5: Poverty in the 21st Century

1. What are some ways that countries in Africa benefit from improved internet access?

2. Explain why some experts believe cell phones might be one key to ending global poverty.

3. Can you think of an invention or service that might benefit people in poverty, either in the United States or in other countries?

4. What are some ways that everyone, poor or not, could benefit from an end to poverty?

Doctors Without Borders

333 7th Avenue, 2nd Floor
New York, NY 10001
(212) 679-6800
www.doctorswithoutborders.org

Doctors Without Borders is an international humanitarian organization that provides aid to people around the world whose lives are threatened by violence, neglect, or natural and man-made disasters.

The Full Belly Project

PO Box 7874
Wilmington, NC 28406
(910) 452-0975
info@thefullbellyproject.org
www.thefullbellyproject.org

The Full Belly Project is involved with the design and distribution of projects to promote sustainable agriculture in developing countries.

Heifer International

1 World Avenue
Little Rock, AR 72202
(855) 948-6437
www.heifer.org

Heifer International works with families and individuals to generate income from the donation of livestock such as one cow or a couple of chickens. People donate money for specific projects they wish to support.

Oxfam International

226 Causeway Street, 5th Floor
Boston, MA 02114
(800) 776-9326
info@oxfamamerica.org
www.oxfam.org

> Oxfam is a group of non-governmental organizations from three continents that work to promote human rights and reduce worldwide poverty.

Volunteers of America

1660 Duke Street
Alexandria, VA 22314
(703) 341-5000
www.voa.org

> Through this volunteering organization, people can donate their time or money to help Americans who live in poverty.

Books

Duck, Waverly. *No Way Out: Precarious Living in the Shadow of Poverty and Drug Dealing*. Chicago, IL: University of Chicago Press, 2015.

> When Waverly Duck was called to be an expert witness in the trial of drug dealer Jonathan Wilson, his stay in Wilson's hometown led him to conduct a long-term study on the ways poverty and crime are related.

Hatcher, Daniel L. *The Poverty Industry: The Exploitation of America's Most Vulnerable Citizens*. New York, NY: New York University Press, 2016.

> This book offers suggestions for welfare reform in the United States.

Lupton, Robert D., and Patrick G. Lawlor. *Toxic Charity: How Churches and Charities Hurt Those They Help (and How to Reverse It)*. Old Saybrook, CT: Tantor Media, 2015.

> Written by an urban activist, this book explores ways to make direct aid more helpful.

Nazario, Sonia. *Enrique's Journey*. New York, NY: Random House, 2006.

> This is the story of a boy's dangerous journey from Honduras to the United States to find his mother, an experience that gives voice to the desperation of poor people in Latin America who risk their lives and the lives of their children in an attempt to climb out of poverty.

Smith, D. Mark. Just One Planet: *Poverty, Justice and Climate Change*. Warwickshire, UK: Intermediate Technology, 2006.
> This book identifies the link between climate change and poverty and makes it clear that the nearly 3 billion people who live on less than $2 per day are most vulnerable to change in patterns of rainfall, river flow, flooding, and drought.

Steinman, Karen. *Poverty*. Philadelphia, PA: Mason Crest, 2017.
> This book explores why poverty exists, how it affects people, and what can be done about it.

Tierney, William G., ed. *Rethinking Education and Poverty*. Baltimore, MD: Johns Hopkins University Press, 2015.
> This collection of essays by experts discusses how education is one key to reducing poverty.

Websites

Free Rice
www.freerice.com
> Free Rice is a nonprofit website run by the United Nations World Food Programme. The website offers visitors multiple-choice quizzes in a variety of subject areas and levels of difficulty. Each correct answer results in the donation of 10 grains of rice to hungry people.

Globalization 101
www.globalization101.org
> This website explores many of the current controversies surrounding globalization.

Our World in Data: Global Extreme Poverty

ourworldindata.org/extreme-poverty

> With statistics and charts, this website explains the facts about poverty around the world.

Poverty USA

www.povertyusa.org

> This website includes statistics, personal stories, and ways individuals can get involved to combat poverty.

UNICEF: Voices of Youth

www.voicesofyouth.org

> The purpose of this website is to educate young people and give them a place to join in discussions, contribute ideas, and become educated about issues relating to poverty. Always ask a parent or guardian before participating in online discussions.

INDEX

PICTURE CREDITS

ABOUT THE AUTHOR

Meghan Sharif is a writer and avid reader. When her nose is not in a book, she works full-time as a teacher for adults with disabilities. In her free time, she enjoys yoga, crocheting, and kickboxing. She lives in Central Pennsylvania.